MIGUEL DE UNAMUNO:
THE CONTRARY SELF

Frances Wyers

MIGUEL DE UNAMUNO: THE CONTRARY SELF

TAMESIS BOOKS LIMITED

LONDON

Colección Támesis: SERIE A, MONOGRAFIAS, LXI

© by Tamesis Books Limited, London, 1976

ISBN 0 7293 0025 0

Designed and printed by
The Compton Press Ltd.
The Old Brewery
Tisbury, Wilts

for

TAMESIS BOOKS LIMITED
LONDON

Contents

For Carlos Blanco Aguinaga

ACKNOWLEDGEMENT

I wish to express my gratitude to the Horace H. Rackham School of Graduate Studies, University of Michigan, for support in the publication of this book.

F.W.

Introduction: The Divided Self

> Reading the work of Pascal . . . one is invited not
> to study a philosophy but to know a man.
>
> (*La agonía del cristianismo*)

Miguel de Unamuno (1864-1936), Spanish essayist, novelist, poet, philosopher, is an exemplary figure in our age. The violent contradictions of his thought reflect and predict the violent contradictions of our culture. The frenzied shifts and turns of his conceptual formulations are a model of contemporary intellectual disjunction and splintered feelings. His doubts about his own existence, his frantic pursuit of the self, and the loneliness of that solipsistic quest, have come to be the common experience of many. Unamuno's works give a vivid picture of the sense of separation and frightening isolation that are central and pervasive themes in modern literature. Although Unamuno denied (sometimes by a paradoxical affirmation) and obfuscated his internal conflicts, he was often enough aware of his evasive strategies; his writings constitute an extensive and almost lucid record of internal cleavage. His destructive passions have found many enthusiastic admirers and angry detractors. The reader who is fascinated by Unamuno (and perhaps also the reader who is repelled by him) responds to the heightened intensity of a familiar emotional and intellectual pattern.

Unamuno was born in Bilbao, the youngest of the four children of Felix Unamuno and his wife (who was also his niece), Salomé de Jugo. His father, a merchant, had spent several years in Mexico and had returned to Spain with some money and a small library. He died when Unamuno was five and the boy retained only a few dim memories, though one stood out, as he once wrote, "in the blurred remembrance of the mists" : one day he slipped into the living-room where his father was speaking French with a visitor; that different language was both a surprise and a discovery : "the mystery of language must have been a great revelation for me. A philologist's vocation !"[1]

Other significant memories were of long country walks with his father which instilled in him a life-long love of nature and which he always considered his most fruitful lessons, "the living rock of my inner culture".[2] Yet in his work this first culture was never fully integrated with the one acquired later, the culture of reason and language. Nature and man remained separated in most of his

---

[1] *Recuerdos de niñez y mocedad* (Buenos Aires: Austral, 1952), pp. 9-10.
[2] Margaret Rudd, *The Lone Heretic, A Biography of Miguel de Unamuno* (Austin: University of Texas Press, 1963), p. 22.

writings; he exiled landscape from his fictions and then made it the exclusive subjects of poems, essays, and travel books. Unamuno's thought plays itself out in antithetical pairs – heart/head, substance/form, reality/appearance, inner/outer, masculine consciousness/feminine unconsciousness – that are rarely, if ever, experienced as the opposing poles of a single continuum. The one is always the negation of the other. Nature and history are mutually exclusive terms.

Unamuno was an introspective child, at first extremely quiet, though he soon developed into a talkative and rather pedantic person; one biographer applies to him this description of the autobiographical hero of his first novel. "He talked a lot but it was always as though from within, bothering a lot of people who thought him tiresome and pedantic because he always wanted to monopolize the conversation, stubbornly picking up where he left off whenever he was interrupted. Then too, they sensed that, treating the listener as an abstraction and engrossed within himself, his conversations were nothing more than pretexts for his monologues and other people mere geometrical shapes, samples of humanity which he treated *sub speciae aeternitatis*. For his part, he was greatly worried about what other people thought about him, for it hurt him if they judged him ill, and he tried hard to be liked and understood by everybody, for he was deeply concerned with the idea that others had of him."[3] This concern with his image in the eyes of others is one of the motive forces of his entire work.

Among sisters and brothers there existed a pattern of intense antipathies countered by a single idealized alliance. He did not get along at all with his oldest sister, María (ten years his senior); throughout the twenty-three years that she spent in his household in Salamanca, the two rarely spoke directly to each other. Nor was much love lost between Miguel and his older brother Félix. But the second child, Susana, who became a nun, he "adored". Unamuno always thought of historical events in terms of the conflicts of family life; the second Carlist War (he had witnessed the seige of Bilbao when he was nine) was for him a paradigm of all wars – the fraternal struggle between Cain and Abel. The theme of brotherly hate and envy inspired much of his fiction.

The family was devoutly Catholic and the deeply religious mother nurtured her son's devotion. He attended mass daily as a child and began his study of philosophy in orthodox Catholic writers like Balmes and Donoso Cortés; through them he learned of Kant, Fichte, Hegel, and tried to grasp ideas that "produced vertigo in my young and groping mind". Philosophy represented a way out of the immediate world; as he said, he "preferred the poetry of the abstract, to the poetry of the concrete".[4] Through Balmes he acquired a taste for mathematics. On the other side, however, were his love of nature, his admiration for the romantic Basque poet Trueba, and a fascination with his own national roots, the history and legends of the Basques. At fourteen he went through what he called his first spiritual crisis, "the soul's entrance into puberty", when he would "weep for no reason", and believed himself "the object of a premature mysticism". The crisis culminated in a kind of mystical rapture. "I was seized by such an unaccountable anguish that I began to weep without

[3] Rudd, p. 42.
[4] Rudd, p. 37.

knowing why . . . it was the countryside that in silence whispered life's mystery to my heart."[5]

At sixteen Unamuno went to the University of Madrid to study philosophy. There, by his own description, he tried to rationalize his faith and find the Christian spirit underneath the Catholic letter; the effort undermined his faith and one day he stopped going to mass. He plunged into "a heady race through philosophy" – Hegel, Kant, Spencer. But the turning away from Catholicism left him with an enormous need for success and applause; no longer believing in Christian immortality, he sought in "name, fame, and vainglory, a miserable copy of it".[6] He tried, thereafter, to replace religious belief with literary production and renown.

In Madrid Unamuno was also exposed to the current debate on "the Spanish problem", a kind of national identity crisis being aired in newspapers, journals, and public speeches by politicians, intellectuals, and men of letters. Faced with the growing power of Europe's middle classes and the colonizing and expansionist thrusts of foreign capital, the Spaniards were engaged in a family quarrel on how best to divide and use their own shrinking inheritance. They liked to think they were dealing with purely spiritual matters – beliefs, customs, ideologies – but the quarrel revealed a conflict of other interests, between those who wanted to preserve traditional privileges and power (the "casticistas", who defended national "purity") and those who were demanding full participation for Spain in the life of European capitalism (the liberals who argued for "europeanization"). The threat from below to both groups from the working class and the rural proletariat was also clearly evident. Indeed, the identity debate served in part to obscure the real dissensions of the age. The writers who came to be called the "Generation of 1898" (in commemoration of the end of the Spanish empire) – Azorín, Baroja, Unamuno, Maeztu, Antonio Machado – reacted to that threat with an initial sympathy for the cause of the exploited and oppressed. They schooled themselves in anarchism and socialism. Yet, as we shall see in Unamuno's development, attention to concrete historical processes gave way to a romantic idealization of poverty and stagnation; the '98 writers (with the important exception of Machado) soon retreated to an evasive subjectivism, an alienated and alienating bourgeois aesthetics.[7] The shift, however, was never complete and each one of those men saw himself torn by contradictions that were as much a reflection of their society as of their individual psychologies. Turning inwards, they found the same instability and wrenching displacements that they sought to avoid in the outside world. Personal history and social history are inseparable, feeding upon and reinforcing each other.

Unamuno wrote his doctoral thesis on the origin and history of the Basques and in 1884 returned to Bilbao where he began his literary career with articles, addressed to a local audience, on the landscape and customs of the Basque

---

[5] Rudd, p. 41.

[6] *Epistolario a Clarín*, ed. Adolfo Alas (Madrid: Ediciones Escorial, 1941), pp. 86-7.

[7] For an excellent account of the relation between social context and literary forms, see Carlos Blanco Aguinaga, *Juventud del 98* (Madrid: Siglo veintiuno, 1970). Also, covering a longer period, Manuel Tuñón de Lara, *Medio siglo de cultura española (1885-1936)* (Madrid: Tecnos, 1970).

country. From 1894 onward he became known to the general Spanish public through articles and books on national and social themes. He also began to study socialism and Marxist thought and between 1894 and 1897 was a regular contributor to the Bilbao socialist weekly, *La Lucha de Clases*.[8] Party because of the influence of his mother and of his wife, he maintained a half-guilty nostalgia for Christian belief (it was only because of his mother, he wrote to a friend, that he did not say many of the things he thought).[9]

When they were both fourteen, Unamuno had made friends with Concepción Lizárraga, the girl he eventually married. He hesitated about marriage for many years, wondering if he should not devote his life to religion (he had taken as prophetic a certain experience during adolescence when he had opened the Bible at the words "Go and preach the gospel to all nations"). Even after he had "rationalized" and lost his faith, he considered remaining celibate so that he could dedicate himself fully to his career as a writer. Celibacy would have been a guarantee of total privacy and total commitment to the development of his thought, of his soul. "For a long time, a stupid egoism made me fear it. I would say to myself, 'goodbye' if I get married. All of the spiritual energy that I expend on her will be lost for my works . . . I used to think what all those monsters of ambition and egoism think: So-and-so, and So-and-so – a whole string of enviable men – were celibates . . . More than once there occurred to me the foolhardy idea that if I have children, the attentions and care I owe them may distract me from the care I owe my ideas."[10] This jealous zeal for his intellectual work never disappeared though he did finally decide that marriage would provide for him a needed "safety valve". He married Concepción Lizárraga in 1891 at the age of twenty-seven.

His wife and his marriage always meant for him a refuge and a consolation, a kind of return home, a way of regaining his own boyhood. "The steady gaze of my wife . . . brings back the cool breezes of my childhood."[11] Through her he could be reborn to childhood, becoming in a sense his own father – or mother (this theme is central in all his work). The wife responded with a life-long maternal devotion. Mother and wife were for Unamuno interchangeable terms. In the play *Soledad,* the protagonist (who is, according to one friend, a faithful portrait of the author) says to his wife, "you are my mother, my wife". In Chapter VII of *Del sentimiento trágico de la vida*, he describes all love on the model of maternal compassion.

Unamuno not only longed for a mother's love but also dreamed of achieving the mother's role; the commonplaces about literary gestation and the pains of artistic childbirth become intensely personal in his writings. Even his mother-

---

[8] See Blanco Aguinaga, op. cit., chap. II; Rafael Pérez de la Dehesa, *Política y sociedad en el primer Unamuno, 1894-1904* (Madrid: Ciencia Nueva, 1966); Elías Díaz, *Revisión de Unamuno* (Madrid: Tecnos, 1968); Geoffrey Ribbans, "Unamuno en 1899: El Proceso de Montjuich y los Anarquistas", in *Niebla y soledad* (Madrid: Gredos, 1971); Unamuno, *Escritos socialistas: Artículos inéditos,* ed. Pedro Ribas (Madrid: Ayuso, 1976).

[9] *Epistolario a Clarín*, p. 86.

[10] Rudd, p. 48, from Hernán Benítez, "La crisis religiosa de Unamuno", *Revista de la Universidad de Buenos Aires*, 3, no. 9 (Jan. Mar., 1949), p. 22. One of Unamuno's short stories ("Los hijos espirituales", 1916) dramatizes that situation.

[11] Rudd, p. 72.

wife could seem to him to be his child; before his marriage he wrote a friend, "Is she not a little boy? . . . a real little boy . . . that is why I like her! . . . This in the soul and body of a woman, is all that I desire and I shall have it".[12] As happens frequently in his fictions, the roles of parent and child, male and female, creator and created, are easily reversed. Still, it was mostly the mother that he sought in his wife. Although they had nine children, he must have remained, in his own eyes, her favorite son.

In 1891 Unamuno was appointed to the chair of Greek at the University of Salamanca. In that city, in 1897, at the age of thirty three, he underwent a profound emotional crisis whose consequences shaped the whole of his life. He described his experience in many intimate letters to friends and kept a diary that records his religious aspirations and severe self-censure.[13] Central to the crisis was a night in March of that year when he awoke in a state of extreme panic, seized by uncontrollable weeping. He was overwhelmed by a terror of annihilation, death, nothingness. Over and over Unamuno described that scene in essays and fictions; his wife's maternal solicitude and her words – "What is it, my son?" – came to stand for an unattainable solace in the face of utter abandonment and loss. Hoping to counter his terrible anxieties, and out of consideration for his wife and his mother, he tried to regain the faith of childhood by practicing routine devotions. When he saw that the effort was "false", he was "seized again by the thirst for glory, the longing to perpetuate himself in history".[14] Unamuno always linked his fear of death with the pursuit of fame.

He continued teaching at the University when he became its rector in 1900. He also devoted himself to his literary career and read voraciously. It is almost impossible to make any summary statement about his intellectual interests because of their vast scope; his readings covered ancient and modern history, biology, psychology, Protestant and Catholic theology, and philosophy (he taught himself Danish in 1901 in order to read Kierkegaard); he knew well the literature – especially the poetry – of France, Italy, Portugal, England, North and South America. Obviously he took quite seriously his own comment that the more books one reads, the less harm they do. In Spanish literature, the *Quixote* was the object of great devotion and countless speculations. Sénancour's *Obermann* was, he said, almost his breviary. He was fond of memoirs and travel books. His own literary production is voluminous – novels, stories, plays,

---

[12] loc. cit.

[13] Among the accounts of this crisis, see Pere Coromines, "La tràgica fi de Miguel de Unamuno", *Revista de Catalunya* 18, no. 83 (Barcelona, Feb., 1938), pp. 155-70; Luis Granjel, *Retrato de Unamuno* (Madrid: Guadarrama, 1957), pp. 147-58; Emilio Salcedo, *Vida de Don Miguel* (Salamanca: Anaya, 1964), pp. 84-9; Diego Catalán, " 'Aldebarán' de Unamuno. De la noche serena a la noche oscura", *Cuadernos de la cátedra Miguel de Unamuno*, 4 (1953), pp. 43-70; Antonio Sánchez Barbudo, *Estudios sobre Unamuno y Machado* (Madrid: Guadarrama, 1959), passim.; Armando Zubizarreta, *Tras las huellas de Unamuno* (Madrid: Taurus, 1960), pp. 111-51. For references to the correspondence of this time see Diego Catalán, "Tres Unamunos ante un capítulo del Quijote", *Cuadernos de la cátedra Miguel de Unamuno*, 16-17 (1966-7), p. 57, note 22. The diary is published as *Diario íntimo* (Madrid: Escelicer, 1970).

[14] *Epistolario a Clarín*, p. 89.

poetry, essays, newspaper articles, and a few books that might be loosely defined as philosophical.

Unamuno was politically active from the beginning of his public career until his death in 1936, but after his early abandonment of socialism, he refused to be identified with any party or movement. For political reasons he was dismissed from his post as rector in 1914. His continuing sharp criticism of the government led, after Primo de Rivera's installation as dictator in 1923, to his exile in 1924. Although he was pardoned after he had spent four months in Fuerteventura in the Canary Islands, Unamuno refused to return to Spain and went into what was to be six years of voluntary exile in France, first in Paris, then in the border town of Hendaye. That action contributed greatly to the growing legend of a polemical and aggressive writer. Burdened by this legend, by the very public image he had worked so hard to create, Unamuno went through a new period of doubt and inner turmoil. The crisis of 1897 found an echo in the lonely Paris exile of 1925. He returned to Spain, triumphantly, in 1930 and resumed his teaching and rectorship in Salamanca, as well as his active intervention in politics.

Unamuno's political position was consistently non-conformist and unorthodox. He opposed both the dictatorship of Primo de Rivera and, during the Second Republic, some of the basic principles and policies of that government. In the thirties he attacked fascism and communism as two forms of dogma, two "dictatorships". His determined irrationalism had resulted, from the beginning of the century, in a growing estrangement from the social reality of Spain. But that irrationalism in no way interefered with his faith in nineteenth-century bourgeois liberalism. Rejecting the socialist model of a just social order, he held onto an ideology that defended the primacy of the freedom of the individual. The individual was, in his characteristic expression, Unamuno himself, and freedom was the "freedom to be myself".[15] In 1931 he was elected to the Spanish Cortes as representative for Salamanca. In his first speech before the Republican parliament, he attacked the demands for autonomy made by Basques and Catalans and spoke of "monarchical Spain", by which he meant not the institution of the monarchy but a unitarian power, with Castilian hegemony. A few months later he inaugurated the academic year at the University in the name of "Her Majesty Spain, one, sovereign, and universal". (The rightists and fascists in the country welcomed this stance; in the first meeting in Salamanca of the Falange in February of 1935 – to which Unamuno was invited and which, to the scandal of many, he attended – the party leaders underlined his role as defender of Spanish unity.)[16] The themes of Spanish continuity and universality (and Castilian supremacy) were central in his first book (*En torno al casticismo*, 1895) where, as we shall see, the problem of Spanish history, formulated as the contrast between the true nature of the country and its "false and delusive tradition", was linked with the problem of personal continuity, formulated as the contrast between the true or inner self and the false

[15] Unamuno, *Obras completas* (Madrid: Afrodisio Aguado, 1958), vol. XI, p. 960. References to this edition will henceforth be made only with volume and page numbers. All translations from Spanish are mine.

[16] Jean Bécarud, *Miguel de Unamuno y la Segunda República* (Madrid: Taurus, 1965).

or deceptive image created by one's words and deeds. And, since the problem of personality invariably appears in his writings as the problem of Unamuno's personality, the psychological theme subsumes the national or political one. Unamuno saw Spain as a metonymical extension of himself.

* * *

Unamuno is considered one of the most important and influential writers of his time in Spain. His works have aroused the enthusiasm and hostility of many of his countrymen. My study involves an evaluation which is best made explicitly; for me he fails as a philosopher and only partially succeeds as a novelist. But his work is significant, both psychologically and historically precisely because it stands as a striking example of the contradictions and delusions of the liberal intellectual, whether idealist or existentialist. Sartre wrote in 1961, in the beginning of his *Critique de la raison dialectique*, that his generation had "rejected the official idealism in the name of 'the tragic sense of life' " and his note explains that the phrase was made popular by Unamuno. "Of course," he adds, "this tragic sense had nothing in common with the true conflicts of our period."[17] Unamuno's response to those conflicts (like that of so many other writers or thinkers) was to mystify them, transforming concrete and objective processes into a timeless and unchanging tragedy of subjectivity. I describe here the elaborate evasiveness of a prose, both discursive and fictional, that seeks to resolve objective contradictions and subjective ambivalences on the level of language alone. My emphasis is on the sleights of hand and conceptual confusions of the essays and on the internal discordances of many of the fictions. We must look at the intellectual and psychological drama played out within each individual work.[18]

One of the most striking features of Unamuno's thought is his apparent inability or unwillingness to come to grips with the feelings that most troubled him. He made much of his religious doubts, his yearning for faith, and his desire for immortality. Contemporary Spanish readers saw the religious question as his principal theme and his present critics continue to describe his thinking in terms of it, though they also draw attention to what Unamuno called the "problem of personality" which becomes more prominent in his later works and which they often point to as evidence of his "existentialist" philosophy. Although religion and the problem of personality are certainly the ostensible

[17] *Search for a Method*, trans. Hazel E. Barnes (New York: Vintage, 1968).

[18] There is no psychologically oriented study of Unamuno's life though it would be a rich subject for investigation. Margaret Rudd's biography provides a concise treatment of much intriguing material. José Luis Abellán, in *Miguel de Unamuno a la luz de la psicología* (Madrid: Tecnos, 1964), makes some interesting observations but his search for "symptoms" or stable features of what he considers Unamuno's neurosis leads him to conceive of personality as a collection of traits instead of an evolving dynamic tension. Moreover, by identifying Unamuno's "true conflict" as that between fame and religious aspiration, he limits it to its most external manifestation. The same more or less stable pattern is presented in A. R. Fernández y González's perceptive study "Unamuno en su espejo", *Boletín de la Biblioteca de Menéndez Pelayo*, 17 (1966), pp. 233-304. Both are versions of the persistent "two-self" theory that I discuss later. Although biographical studies would add much to our understanding of the author, his works themselves should be studied as statements of internal conflict.

topics of much of what he wrote, we sense underneath them a personal struggle that does not rise to the level of conscious expression. Unamuno talks a
great deal about faith, doubt, the mystery of the self, the problematic relation
between the real and the fictitious, but one looks in vain for the intellectual
ordering that would tie together these themes in any comprehensible way. Of
course, everyone knows and repeats that Unamuno was not and did not want
to be a systematic philosopher. His often proclaimed aversion to system and
dogma (for him almost synonyms) and his manifest pride in disorder would
seem to tell us that we can hardly fault him for what he quite defiantly chose
not to do.

The opposition to systematization or to strict intellectual patterning could
have taken other forms; Unamuno might have cultivated the kind of playful
subversiveness found in the prose of Antonio Machado or Jorge Luis Borges, or
he might have abandoned the essay entirely and devoted himself to fiction,
theater, and poetry. But he produced a prodigious number of articles and
longer prose works of a loosely philosophical nature in which, while denying the
value of coherent argument, he tries to convince the reader of the truth of what
he says. Although we should not ignore the purely economic side of this pro-
ductivity (that most Spanish writers relied heavily on the fees paid by journals
and newspapers must be considered in any evaluation of the prose of the
period), Unamuno apparently also felt a great personal need to communicate
with his readers through this medium. He clearly conceived of his essays (and
of all his literature) as a way of baring his soul and exposing to others his inmost desires and torments. Because he saw the essay as an emotional outpouring
he naturally took very few pains in its construction; they all more or less follow
the principle of the one titled "A lo que salga" – the rule of chance. He composed with a determined disregard for structure and coherence; frequently
enough, one can scarcely find any single unifying topic so that the title seems
an arbitrary afterthought. The reader of Unamuno's essays is plunged into a
chaos of paradoxical affirmations and negations; he feels he cannot touch
ground or find any path to a clearing in the tangle of prose. Eventually it becomes evident that all the conceptual shifts and turns obey principles that are
never enunciated. Nothing can be taken at face value and we must search for
an undisclosed fabric of meaning that the author seems to be almost purposely
obfuscating. So the soul-baring and the exhibitionist stance is also a cover-up;
the actor, as Unamuno says in one of his essays, acts in order to conceal his true
self.

This simultaneous showing and hiding explains the oddly disjunctive quality
of his writing. True concerns are replaced by an enormous verbal mass that
obscures or, at best, hints at what lies beneath. There is, in other words, a
marked separation between what he talks about and what he says.

This duplicity of style and thought also explains the lack of any genuine
intellectual evolution; what we perceive in its stead is an increasingly complicated psychological division. Although at least one critic goes so far as to
argue that all of Unamuno's contradictions would disappear if we read his
works in strictly chronological order,[19] I see at most a very general shift in em-

---

[19] See Diego Catalán, "Tres Unamunos", p. 38.

phasis. And contradictions abound even in a single essay. Throughout all his works we find a persistent contrariness, an almost desperate need to set up oppositions and then collapse them into a single entity, to take sides and then switch, to deny and then deny the denial or to assert that what was denied was really affirmed. The reader is confounded and ensnared in a rhetoric of perpetual self-reversal.

As for the consistency of his themes, from the 1897 Diary to his death we find him worrying the same ones (he often said that great writers play out only one or two basic themes). Over and over he returns to the same subject. But the consistency is a mere surface phenomenon because his concepts and verbal images continually alter; a careful reading of the texts shows that a single word or topic may represent a series of significations that are often mutually exclusive. These continual transmutations give his language a curiously autonomous quality, as if certain key phrases at one moment set in motion one train of thought, at another, one that is quite distinct. The intellectual coherence that many of his admirers like to find in his works rests on this verbal illusion. The same words are set to quite different tunes which sometimes are played simultaneously in an essay so that one must imagine two or more intersecting scores.

The critics who have discussed the contradictory nature of his writings have either explained it in terms of a rationalist/mystical dichotomy in his personality, attributable to a biographical event (the loss of faith during his university years) or have spoken of hypocrisy and inauthenticity. The first approach supposes good faith and takes Unamuno's famous tragic sense of life quite seriously; the second presents us with a man quite consciously bent on deception who parades his anguish for theatrical effect, a man who would win an audience by any means in order, as Unamuno once wrote, "to be seen, admired, and leave a name". In a way both are correct. But I think a more accurate description would be of a self-deceiving consciousness that does not recognize the true roots of its despair. Thus the critics who turn Unamuno's existential conflict into an existentialist philosophy confuse the symptom with its philosophical formulation. Most of Unamuno's prose makes clear what Sartre meant by "bad faith".

Yet Unamuno himself appears to recognize his elaborate and devious facade for what it is. "I never reveal my thinking more clearly to myself than when I am trying to conceal it." Self-deception would here seem to become a means of self-disclosure. And it is, in a sense. But what he conceals, as I hope to show in an examination of the essays, is not really the same thing as what he reveals; there is always a gap between the confession and the hidden thought. The same might be said of Unamuno's well-known fondness for paradox. Unamuno's paradoxes are the result of an unexamined, almost frantic, effort to tie together opposing aspirations. They are expressions of an emotional ambivalence that he would pass off in the guise of an intellectual riddle. This becomes evident when, as so often happens, the paradox suddenly dissolves and one term is absorbed into its opposite. Coalescence replaces contradiction.

Even when he talks about his own contradictions, his attitude changes strikingly from text to text. At one point he calls himself a "heutontimoroumenos" who spends his life trying to be what he is not, without succeeding. He quotes St. Paul, "I do not the good that I would, but the evil I would not do".

Yet six years later he wrote, "If I ever write a history of my thought . . . I will show how continuous, how consistent it has been" (*O.C.*, III, 1063). More than once he comes to the point of asserting that inconsistency is the mark of true inward stability ("Sobre el fulanismo", "Sobre la consecuencia, la sinceridad"). What, one keeps wondering, is really going on?

In *Del sentimiento trágico de la vida*, and in several other places as well, Unamuno wrote that the inner biography of a man is what explains most about his philosophy (XVI, 128). We do not have to look far in Unamuno's life for the emotional correlates of these conceptual gyrations. Unamuno was very much aware of the discontinuities in his own life and they evidently caused him considerable uneasiness. He had been a Christian and then an agnostic. The socialist concerned with the problems of this world suddenly found himself looking for consolation in the other. The failure to achieve it sent him once more in search of renown. At any moment in this series of transformations he could not help but remember that he had felt otherwise, that he was, as he so often said, "el otro", the other, another – the rationalist or the Catholic. And, he always added, if one is another, he is not himself. Being another means "ceasing to be". Change, for Unamuno, is a kind of death.

One might take the biographical considerations a little further back. We move beyond available information and into the zone of speculation. Unamuno must have experienced very early in life an intense insecurity about his very being. His works show us a man who seems to doubt that he is there at all. In an effort to counter that frightful possibility he seeks to affirm the solidity of his self, his personality. Throughout his writings he speaks of an inner substance, an inner core, and his language is colored with nostalgia and longing. When he claims that the soul is the most substantial part of a man and that the body is a mere husk or shell, he expresses a disdain for the visible and the concrete in favor of an invisible "concreteness" that can exist nowhere. But that impossible substance is exactly what he aims at – his own substance, his own inner core. Unamuno tried constantly to grasp his own self. He imagines it as something stable and solid. Characteristically he thinks of it in physical terms, firm as bedrock, yet sensually inviting and throbbing with life. He speaks of searching out one's soul and embracing it, rubbing up against it and feeling its substance and warmth. Although this never quite becomes an explicit topic, it is clear that he seeks union with himself, a kind of magical self-copulation in a hidden and invisible place. Behind Unamuno's preferences for certain gut words – blood, bones, marrow, palpitating entrails – stands a private mythology about a secret world to which he longs to gain access and a secret substance which is his very own.

Inner reality also represents a refuge from the external world. He escapes inwards. But Unamuno is even less explicit about this aspect of his goal. Indeed, nowhere does he fully describe for his readers the notion of the inner self; one must piece it together on the basis of passages scattered throughout his work. It is not part of an intellectual scheme but a kind of wishful fantasy that appears in moments of need. Unamuno developed no psychological theory but he did dramatize – sometimes as if unaware – the essential features of his own psychic life.

The need to take possession of his self also found a contrary form – the outward self that Unamuno longed to get hold of and to see ("If one could only see oneself from without!" he wrote in his Diary). He lusted for fame not so much in order to perpetuate himself as to acquire a visible and tangible self. He would become his own legend. He would make himself an image in the eyes of others and then get back this reflection – a pseudo-substance – in their admiring looks. He thought he could achieve an identity in and through his readers. But the legendary self is visible; it exists in the world subject to the judgements of others, and we have seen that one of the functions of the notion of inwardness is protection from the external world and, ultimately, from the gaze of others. What is visible and external can be appropriated by others; the legend can turn out to be a way of losing the self. Usually Unamuno's search for fame calls up the counter-movement of retreat inwards. But he cannot long be satisfied with what is, after all, only an imaginary internal substance. So he veers from one to the other.

Longing for something solid and unchangeable, Unamuno searches for a self, sometimes within, sometimes without. To the flux and uncertainty of experience he opposes the notion of stability and permanence. Yet the fulfillment of either wish would also mean its destruction. A totally private self has no contact with the world and, as a pure subjectivity, loses the very "substance" that is craved; a self created through fame becomes detached from the life that feeds it. In both cases the image he pursues alienates him from lived experience – from himself and from others. Unamuno's wishes only heighten the fear of the void. In the Diary he several times described his terror of non-being as a consequence of the aim of self-possession. "Would not an eternity of solitude, alone with one's void, be more horrible than nothingness? Since you have thought only of yourself and searched only for yourself . . . you will be with yourself and only yourself for all eternity, with your inner world, your senses closed to the external one, and thus you will sink into your own nothingness and have it for eternal company."[20] Realizing full well that the fixity he dreamed of could exist only outside of life, he feared it at the same time that he wished for it. The fear sometimes pushed him to a complete self-renunciation; then he longed to lose himself in his people or his readers, in nature, in eternity, in God, in unconsciousness. Death would be his mother and his bride (the protagonist's vision at the end of the play El hermano Juan).

Two patterns of oscillation can be traced in his works, the one including the other : the first alternates between, on the one hand, the search for a solid inner core and, on the other, the wish to grasp the self as an image in the eyes of others; the second moves between the dream of self-possession and the dream of self-dissolution. He sometimes desires the very thing he most fears. The feeling of alienation makes him long for union, yet the dread of being submerged by the world (or God) sends him back in pursuit of a lonely and constricted identity. This double set of reversing mechanisms is in perpetual motion because each wish inevitably calls up its contrary.

Unamuno was aware of his inner division but he was not aware of its true

[20] *Diario*, pp. 133-4. Also, "this obsession with nothingness, is it not pure egotism?" (p. 230). See also pp. 229 and 247.

polarities nor of the way they functioned in his thoughts and feelings. Instead of confronting the specific nature of his contradictions, he described them in terms that were much in fashion among the '98 writers in their discussions of the crisis of Spanish culture and the problem of national personality; he spoke of the dichotomy between action and contemplation. "These are my two great longings, action and repose. I have within me, and doubtless all men do, two men, one active, and one contemplative, one warlike and one pacific, one enamored of agitation, the other of calm" (IV, 55-6). What Unamuno does here is make use of a ready-made formula that has very little to do with the complicated shifts between the fear of insubstantiality, the craving for personal substance or external image and the opposite self-negating desire for dissolution and absorption. Nor does he come any closer to an accurate picture of his dramatic imbalance in his many references to the war between reason and sentiment, heart and head: "I do not want to find inner peace in harmonies, concordances, and compromises that lead to inert stability; I do not want my heart to make peace with my head, but both to do battle with each other . . . I am, and want to continue to be, an antinomic, dualistic spirit . . . my whole life moves by a principle of inner contradiction."[21] This description too simplifies and displaces the real contradiction and turns it into a romantic duel between equally respected antagonists. The claim that he shuns peace and harmony is typical of Unamuno's continual effort to make his suffering a proof of his solidity, strength, and superiority, an effort which underlies the whole conception of *Del sentimiento trágico de la vida*. The apparent and prideful acceptance of the inner war is, however, belied by every page in which Unamuno attempts to fuse contraries and to turn reality into a dream-like fiction.

The action/contemplation duality has provided several critics with a model of psychological division; they speak of an "agonic" and a contemplative Unamuno or of a man who retained in some way his childhood religious faith while professing publicly his doubts; they refer to a clash between an original disposition (what Unamuno always referred to as his childhood self) and a subsequent intellectual and/or histrionic development.[22] These critics see a basic stratum of personality overlaid with contrary attitudes and they do not move beyond the fact of alternating positions. But the supposedly underlying childhood self, the contemplative one, is clearly as much a creation of Unamuno's fears and internal opposition as the self that seeks its confirmation in fame. Indeed, Unamuno's whole concern with religion must have sprung out of the need to support an originally precarious sense of being. Everything that he wrote about God, from the Diary to *La agonía del cristianismo*, indicates that his principal concern was finding some guarantee for personal immortality. God's primary if not only function for Unamuno is the maintenance and per-

---

[21] Quoted by A. R. Fernández y González, op. cit., p. 290.

[22] The most well-known formulation is Blanco Aguinaga's *El Unamuno contemplativo* (México: Colegio de México, 1959). See also the works cited by Zubizarreta, Sánchez Barbudo, Catalán, Fernández y González. Sánchez Barbudo (op. cit.) emphasizes the histrionic quality of Unamuno's anguish. François Meyer (*La ontología de Miguel de Unamuno*, tr. C. Goicoechea, Madrid: Gredos, 1962) gives an admirable analysis of Unamuno's ontology of conflict but he does not carry that interpretation over to the conception or experience of the self on which, contrary to his belief, the ontology is based.

petuation of individual existence. The faith he lost must have itself evolved out of an early and great fear of non-being. Its loss aggravated an already desperate need.

Unamuno's works do not show us an "agonic" writer who sometimes slips into a prior mode but a person who veers ceaselessly between mutually exclusive and ultimately self-defeating aims. Yet the contrary aims have a common root – the fear of insubstantiality, a primary doubt about the very existence of the self. It is this common root which makes inevitable the frenzied and dizzying fluctuations. Dreading annihilation he devises protective images that turn out to menace him with the very destruction he flees from. So he darts back and forth among them, sometimes shifting course in the middle of an argument or jumping from one level of opposition (inner self/outer self) to the other (possession of self/loss of self).

Of course Unamuno knew very well his terror of nothingness; he referred to it over and over. He made it the core of his book *Del sentimiento trágico de la vida* in which his personal dilemma is elevated to an ontological conflict. Yet though he says there that every philosophy has its roots in the author's emotional life, he does not really describe the concrete connections between his own feelings and their conceptualizations. Instead, he remains on the level of general emotional antitheses – reason and sentiment, heart and head, and, more ominously, "all or nothing". Unamuno is unable to make explicit the links between his fears and the ideological and verbal maneuvers employed to overcome them.

The strategies are apparent but they do not seem to be controlled by the author. Unamuno talks about his pain, but the causes of that pain surface on their own; they become evident in spite of him, in spite of the intended or apparent thrust of his declarations. What I shall describe in his works are certain patterns of which the writer himself seems largely unaware. The "exposition" I offer of a given essay or book is not, I believe, the one that Unamuno would have made. The messages I perceive are not the ones consciously elaborated by Unamuno. I am looking for the arguments that run beneath, though not always very far beneath, the surface of the texts.

In his fictional works Unamuno seems in general clearer about his own meanings. Yet many of them too reveal strange cross purposes and apparent reversals; his own comments about them in prefaces or subsequent references are sometimes totally disconcerting because they express attitudes which run counter to those that emerge from the fictions themselves.

That Unamuno became such an important figure in the Hispanic world is due in part to the relative isolation of Spanish from European culture since the seventeenth century. He brought before Spain's small reading public certain central intellectual and existential concerns of the late nineteenth and early twentieth centuries. It is true that he wrote about them in the somewhat anachronistic language of religious faith and doubt and that when he approached "the problem of personality" his own egocentricity (which he always defended) sometimes obscured the real philosophical issues. The most serious failing of his work is its complicated deviousness; yet that is also one source of its interest. Unamuno the thinker and essayist gives way to Unamuno as a personality that embodies and dramatizes certain contemporary modes of intellectual and emotional disjunction. He is neither the first nor the last writer to formulate a mystique of inwardness and to deal with the contrary pulls between an inaccessible inner truth and the deceits of actions aimed only at impressing others. His work is best viewed as what Unamuno himself called an "exemplary novel".

PART ONE
ESSAYS

I

The Inner Self and the External Self

There is no direct intuition of the self that is worth anything; the eye cannot see itself except in a mirror and the mirror of moral man is found in his works, of which he is the offspring. (III, 195, *En torno al casticismo*, 1895)

A man does not know himself except in the same way that he knows others. He sees himself act and . . . deduces what he is like . . . No one, in reality, knows himself a priori, before he acts; all of us know ourselves in our own actions, which are often enough foreign to us. (III, 96, "De la enseñanza superior en España", 1899)

Introspection is very deceptive and, carried to an extreme, produces a true void in consciousness . . . Because a state of consciousness that would consist purely and simply in consciousness contemplating itself, would not, for lack of content, be any kind of consciousness at all. . . . We learn to know ourselves in the same way that we learn to know others : by observing our actions. (III, 617-18, "El individualismo español", 1902)

In these passages Unamuno denies that there is any duality in human consciousness. No secret self hides behind one's actions. Each person creates himself in his words and deeds. Nor is there any privileged mode of apprehending the self; introspection provides no real knowledge. Statements like these reappear frequently enough in later years, but they are most typical of Unamuno's thought prior to the crisis of 1897. During that period most of his writings focused on the social and political problems of Spain : he examined its past and speculated about its future. In *En torno al casticismo* (as well as in "El individualismo español" and other early essays) he talked about self-knowledge in order to make an analogy to historical knowledge.[1]

Yet in those same works, alongside the claims of consciousness through action, are references to an inner, submerged reality composed of "eternal truths of eternal essence" and apparently independent of history. In *En torno al casticismo (On "Casticism"*, II, 155-303), Unamuno compares this "eternal tradition" to the silent depths of the sea. The historical is the surface of the sea

---

[1] Unamuno's interest in Spain and his interest in the problem of personality became increasingly identified. As Elías Díaz has observed, he tended to see himself as the personal embodiment of his country. "Characteristically the symbiosis Unamuno-Spain reaches the point of an authentic and total identification, a mutual transfer of reciprocal problems. Unamuno finally saw himself as a miniature Spain and Spain as a magnified Unamuno; the essence of each being . . . contradictory, agonic, in eternal and endless inner warfare" (*Revisión de Unamuno*, p. 100).

crystalized and congealed in books, papers, and monuments; underneath is the silent life of millions of men without history who perform their obscure "daily and eternal tasks". Unamuno had said he was writing the book to show how Spain had "formed and revealed itself in History" and to demonstrate how its past reveals the unvarying characteristics of an enduring pattern, but he frequently sets history and tradition against each other. The former is the record of people who act and "make noise" and whose works constitute a "false and delusive tradition", while the latter, which Unamuno called "intrahistory", is the unrecorded and unchanging culture of the peasants. Unamuno postulates an archetypal Spanish personality unmodified by events in time. He even goes so far as to warn against confusing the inner nature of a people with the form it acquires as it passes from "the realm of freedom to the realm of history". In this, Unamuno joins other members of the Generation of 1898 who saw the history of Spain as a deformation of its true character.[2]

Unamuno repeatedly formulates this dichotomy between inner truth and external façade and he repeatedly dissolves it. Oppositions are posited and negated and the contrary lines of an argument cross and recross. Thus although the metaphors of living depths and frozen surfaces suggest mutually uncommunicating zones Unamuno states that "intrahistory" is both the source and the sediment of history, its origin and its product. He thereby attempts to fuse the historical and the eternal into a single concept ("the daily eternal") that really absorbs the one into the other.[3] Contraries are resolved, not in paradox, which would preserve the antithetical nature of each, but in verbal coalescence : you call one thing by the name of its opposite.

These reversals of affirmation and negation characterize everything that Unamuno wrote about the self. As his attention turned from national topics to psychological ones, the tension between his need to separate the "true" self from the public one and the contrary need to fuse them, becomes increasingly evident.

It is not difficult to find in Unamuno's writings from 1895 to 1905 numerous statements that emphasize the distinction between the inner self and the external one. The latter is denigrated or repudiated; it is mere appearance, a shell or covering that imprisons the true self. In an unpublished novel of 1896 (*Mundo nuevo*) Unamuno lamented the fact that "men are more concerned about their appearance in the minds of others than about the reality within themselves". He spoke scornfully of the external life that, with its noise and distraction, "keeps one from hearing the living silence in the eternal depths of his being".[4] The language is similar to that used in *En torno al casticismo* to

[2] Pedro Laín Entralgo, in *La generación de 1898* (Madrid : Austral, 1947), quotes this letter to Ganivet : "History, wretched History, which is mostly an imposition of the environment, has hidden from us the bed-rock of the country's nature" (p. 146).

[3] Carlos Blanco Aguinaga has called this fusion "an emotional sleight of hand" (*El Unamuno contemplativo*, México; Colegio de México, 1959, p. 189). For a contrary interpretation, see Peter G. Earle, "Unamuno : *historia* and *intra-historia*", in *Spanish Thought and Letters in the Twentieth Century*, ed. Germán Bleiberg and E. Inman Fox (Nashville; Vanderbilt University Press, 1966), pp. 179-86.

[4] Zubizarreta, *Tras las huellas de Unamuno*, p. 76; Diego Catalán, "Tres Unamunos . . .", p. 62.

describe the eternal Spanish character. In the Diary he said that the external self is made by others and by the world – or by oneself in deference to their demands; through our conduct we fabricate a "poor copy of ourselves" in conformity to the opinions of others. Behavior, far from being a clue to the real self, gives only a picture of the false personality that each man imposes upon himself and that "oppresses and smothers our innate being". The "intimate self" and the "historical self" struggle with each other for domination, and only the destruction of the intruder can liberate the real self. In his own case, Unamuno explained that his effort to return to God and the faith of childhood signified the death of the "stage figure" which freed the "real and eternal Miguel that the other one was stifling and oppressing".[5]

Unamuno's endeavour to find a solid unchanging core of personality antedates the crisis of 1897. The only noticeable conceptual change is that, during the crisis and for a short time afterwards, he identified the inner self with the soul created by God. Thus, the "worldly self" will perish but the inner one, "the one lifted out of the void by God, will live in Him". He imagines within himself a concrete entity that can be reached and grasped through Christ. "Seek yourself in the Lord and there you will find true peace and will be able to see yourself face to face, and when you embrace yourself in holy piety, you will feel the permanent substantiality of your soul summoned by Christ to eternal life."[6] In comparison with this substance everything else is phantasmal – especially renown and the esteem of others. In an essay written in 1898 ("La vida es sueño", "Life is a Dream" III, 407-17), Unamuno criticized those people who, having lost faith in the immortality of the soul, seek glory and "the immortalization of our phantom here below."

The radical separation between real and phantasmal and the identification of the first with the religious self are also advanced in "Nicodemo el fariseo" ("Nicodemus the Pharisee", III, 121-54). Unamuno read this address to the Athenaeum of Madrid in 1899 though it was written early the previous year. This was his first public speech in several years and it represented, as he wrote to one of his friends, "a laying bare of the soul".[7] In an improvised introduction he told his audience that he himself was the Pharisee. We must conclude that Nicodemus's search for a solution to the problem of psychological change and identity is Unamuno's own and that Christ's message is the one Unamuno wanted to hear. Nicodemus asks how one can be born again, how transformation is possible if actions are irrevocable and if a man is the result of his life. Christ replies that although acts are irrevocable, intentions are not. We must not confuse the act, which occurs in time, with its root, which is found in eternity; the eternal self is the only one we must attend to. Christ distinguishes between deeds and the faith or impulse that motivates them. The first belong to the

---

[5] *Diario*, pp. 177-80.
[6] *Diario*, pp. 82-3.
[7] Unamuno wrote to his friend Arzadun that this article would scandalize many of his friends and make them call him a retrograde, a mystic, a skeptic, a madman. See Hernán Valenzuela Benítez, *El drama religioso de Unamuno* (Buenos Aires: Universidad de Buenos Aires, Insto. de Publicaciones, 1949), p. 246, note 2; also Catalán, op. cit., p. 63, note 66.

world of mere appearances and are the movements of earthly, not spiritual, man. Nicodemus, Christ says, is misled when he considers only the physical man "who moves and changes in time and appearance and not the one who persists in eternal reality".[8] "Living faith" means more than "dead works". Nicodemus has made the mistake of not looking for the "self that is underneath the self that acts".

At this point in the dialogue the two selves are clearly separable but the one is still the root and source of the other. As Christ continues his argument, the tie between them becomes more tenuous until man is split into two parts increasingly remote from each other. "In all of us . . . there are two men, a temporal one and an eternal one."[9] At birth the spiritual embryo is put into the "womb of the world" and its growth is not only independent from that of the physical self but contrary to it, developing from within outwards, directed by God. There is another growth "from outside in" which deposits a sediment around our "eternal nucleus" and almost drowns it in time. The world threatens to smother the soul in layers of passion, iniquity, and egoism. Men live encased in shells (costras) of varying thickness that isolate them from themselves and from each other.[10] The essay moves towards a complete alienation from the physical self. It is not "me" but the world. "All that dirty crust that was born of the flesh, of the world, is flesh and world; but what was born in you in the spirit, is spirit."[11]

The inner self is the one by which we will ultimately be redeemed or condemned, but it can be known only inwardly; it is hidden from others because its desires are never manifested in action. Unamuno describes will, intention, and desire as the hallmarks of the inner self, but they connect with nothing outside of it. In some statements, he describes action as the antithesis of will because it occurs in time and can be judged by others. "You are a slave in your acts but not in your intentions. When you act, your action is subject to the bonds of all appearances . . . You must look for your freedom not so much in doing as in willing . . . go into the interior of that holy liberty and take refuge there from the tyrannies of the shell of your soul." In separating the deed from the doer and wish from fact, Unamuno proposes a retreat from the world and from the empirical self into a realm of sheer virtuality. In the "inner world" he is something different from what he is in his acts. His true self is always other than what can be observed; it is not the sum of actions or the historical drama

[8] In Unamuno's first novel, *Paz en la guerra*, he describes Pedro Antonio as enjoying "the intimate intensity of a life of work, obscure and silent in the reality of himself and not in the appearance of others" (*Obras completas*, Madrid: Escelicer, 1967, vol. II, p. 78).

[9] Unamuno's Christ extends the dualistic vision of the gospel: "That which is born of the flesh is flesh; and that which is born of the spirit is spirit" (John 3: 6).

[10] In the Diary he identified the *costra* with sin, specifically with the sin of pride, and said that humility breaks the shell and bares the soul (p. 11).

[11] Ricardo Gullón believes that Unamuno was suggesting that the temporal and the eternal should coexist in constant friction. " 'I am nothing but the result of my life', exclaims the existentialist Nicodemus long before Sartre" (*Autobiografías de Unamuno*, Madrid: Gredos, 1964, p. 157). Nicodemus, however, had come to Christ to be cured of such "existentialism"; he wants to be convinced of the alternate possibility, that one's soul is different from the self that exists in time.

6

of possibilities and choices. The real self is forever untouchable and elusive, persisting beyond time as an eternal reservoir of pure intentions.[12]

Unamuno returns to the ideal of a transcendent self in many later essays. In "El secreto de la vida" (1906, III, 1027-42) he speaks of a mystery that each person carries within him "like a terrible and precious tumor". This secret, invisible seed is planted by God, whereas the external personality, which Unamuno calls the foliage of the soul, is shaped by society through the medium of language which conventionalizes private thoughts and feelings. Although the outward self belongs more to the world than to oneself, the mysterious inner source belongs only to the subject. "That sap which cannot be seen, that is mine." Significantly, Unamuno thinks of the center of personality as a possession that must be jealously guarded from prying eyes. One must not expose the "entrails" of spirit to sun and air that would dry and kill them. Since the inner life-source cannot survive the light of day (and the scrutiny of others), Unamuno imagines a dark and sheltering home for it : beneath the visible and noisy world where we rush frantically about there is another "invisible and silent world" of eternal quiescence. In this hidden place "freedom is buried and grows inwards, not outwards". To escape the objective world of words and deeds Unamuno constructs a fantastic one where the self can be totally autonomous – in silence and repose.

In "Sobre la consecuencia, la sinceridad" ("Before Consistency, Sincerity", 1906, III, 1034-64), Unamuno contrasts the inner self to the social one in order to examine the problem of psychological continuity. Each person is at least two different persons, "a deep, radical, permanent self, which many now call subliminal . . . beneath the level of consciousness, and another superficial, stuck on, and ephemeral". He talks of them as if they functioned independently, the outer one giving no hint as to the make-up of the inner one. Since the subject must filter his thoughts and feelings through the language of the others, using "superficial ideas and logical concepts", he inevitably misrepresents himself. Subjectivity is always hidden. Unamuno argues that we cannot make a judgement about the consistency or sincerity of another person on the basis of his expressed ideas and values because consistency is often only a sign of hypocrisy and deference to others. True inward continuity might very well manifest itself in the most contrary ways (as he said in another place, men are much more reliable than their ideas – "Sobre el fulanismo", III, 633-53). Unamuno was eager to slip free of any conclusions his readers may have made about his own contradictory positions. "Do not let them classify me", he kept saying. He wanted to hide from the summary opinion that would, to his mind, steal his self from him. "Let them search for you and do not let them find you because the day that they find you, you are no longer yourself" (V, 991).

One of Unamuno's favorite analogies for psychological complexity was based

[12] Contradicting the extreme dualism of this essay is a passage in the introduction that points to an integration of spirit and flesh. "The economic and the religious are the two hinges of human history. The so-called materialist conception of life, Marx's . . . shows us only one face of reality, the external . . . the other is the one we could call the spiritualist conception . . ." (III, 123). The whole thrust of the article, however, negates this observation.

on a passage from Oliver Wendell Holmes about how each person was really three, "Juan as he is, Juan as he thinks he is and Juan as others think he is" (III, 1049). Unamuno sometimes expanded this scheme to a multiplicity of of social roles – every man is really many different ones, "the solitary man is legion". From the actions and reactions of our several selves, "from the way the idea I have of myself influences the idea others have, and vice versa, the ideal self lives and develops" (XI, 330). Although this might suggest that the self is, as one critic says, a "vertiginous becoming",[13] we begin to suspect that it is really a means of concealment when we find, in the very next paragraph, this assertion : "There is a fourth Juan . . . who is neither the one he is, nor the one he thinks . . . He is the one he wants to be." That self might be forever invisible and a person might die without its being revealed; even so, one is saved or condemned "not for what he was or thought he was but for what he wanted to be" (333). The real self is located beyond the boundaries and bounds of life in the realm of pure desire. "The one we want to be and not the one we are is our intimate self" (X, 531). Even when such statements stand side by side with their negation ("the inner man, the eternal one, is the child of his deeds", X, 534), the general argument of the essay points to the ideal of uncommitted self sufficiency.

Against the changefulness of lived experience, Unamuno aims at impossible continuity and concreteness. He dissociates from his empirical self in order to win total freedom and control for the inner self. But it is precisely this split that makes him resent his bondage. If the external self is not really his, its very existence and objectivity threaten him. Yet he cannot be rid of the false self because it is his body and his history. So he feels constantly imposed upon; he is always in danger of being smothered by the mask, the shell. His language betrays the futility of his efforts : the "dirty crust" is part of him and no matter how hard he tries to cast it off, he finds it "stuck on". The false self may be ephemeral and the real one eternal, but here and now they are yoked together. In "Sobre la consecuencia" he says that the original Juan is often a prisoner of the Juan others have fabricated. "The various concepts our neighbors have of us . . . fall upon our spirit and finally surround it with a kind of carapace, a hard shell, a thick crust" (III, 1049).

So thoroughly is he fused with what he likes to think of as an externally imposed self, that only death can liberate him. In the Diary he said that suicide is often simply a frantic attempt to "free oneself from oneself". "The suicide wants to rid himself, not of life, but of his self." He later speaks of his personal fascination with self-destruction.[14] If one splits oneself in two, suicide can be seen as the murder of the self that does not meet one's image of perfection. In one of his essays, Unamuno calls the external self the murderer of the true one (IX, 899).

The creation of what was meant to be a consoling illusion comes full circle and turns against its author. Unamuno tells his reader that he is not what he seems to be or what he reveals in his writings; he is something finer and purer

[13] Jorge Enjuto, "Sobre la idea de la nada en Unamuno", La Torre, 9, 35-6 (1961), p. 268.

[14] Diario, pp. 82 and 230.

than the limited human being who writes, contradicts himself, changes his mind, says some foolish things, etc. The advantages are obvious – a marvelously clear conscience, protection from the judgements of others and a total, god-like freedom. No one can intrude upon the inner space; no one can see his true face; no one can steal his inward self. He is perfectly defended against everyone – except his own wretched and traitorous "worldly" self, that is, his own concrete existence. Unamuno takes the repudiation of that embodied life to the point of total self-alienation. He sees himself as his own most murderous enemy. The strategy that was devised to shield the inner self ends by destroying it. He has made his body into a double and, as we shall see, in Unamuno's fictions (as in most such stories) the encounter with the double is fatal.

*   *   *

The fantasy of inner substance is paired in Unamuno's writings with the illusion of the self made visible in the eyes of others. What he wanted from his literary public was his own reflected image. In the Diary he wrote that he had often wished that he could see himself from the outside (p. 174). The two goals are always connected. When Unamuno preaches the doctrine of the inner self he condemns exhibitionism. During the crisis of 1897 he accused himself of trying to get fame by any means, even by showing off his moral infirmities; he prided himself on his self-obsession and called attention to it "like those poor wretches at the side of the road who display their sores . . . like children who delight in any injury and . . . pretend to be sicker than they are" (*Diario*, pp. 274-5). Tormented by the thought that his efforts to achieve Christian humility may be only the round-about strategy of pride, he returned over and over in the Diary to what he called his "secret delectation" in suffering – "spiritual masturbation" (pp. 178, 277, 286, 297).

But even when he renounces fame and vainglory, he does not give up hope for immortality here below. In those passages where he scorns ambition, he shifts the locus of his true identity; he still wants perpetuation, but of the inner self and not the external image. In an early story, "Una visita al viejo poeta" ("A Visit to the Old Poet", 1899, II, 745-51), the protagonist says that fame, which is our reflection in the myriad mirrors of our fellow men, threatens to stifle the real self that "comes out of our deepest bowels . . . that sings the pure song of distant childhood". He does not want to sacrifice that self to his name but to anchor it "in the silence of eternity" and that, paradoxically enough, means impressing others with his ideas and persisting in their memory. When the old poet speaks of merging his spirit with that of his people, he is aiming at another kind of immortality; "a writer is often most influential when he is least discussed." The original goal is not renounced but cast in a new form.

The protagonist of "Don Martín o de la gloria" ("D. M. or On Glory", 1900, IX, 160-5) is a famous writer who vigorously rejects this kind of communal or impersonal salvation. He complains that the fame of his books has obscured his own personality; since he has become a classic, no one talks about him anymore. He has "descended into the depths of his people's memories", but he would rather be on the surface because his spirit has diffused itself in that of his readers, it is no longer his; they have robbed him of his self – "I am not mine."

Far from being consoled by the survival of his works, he is tortured by the thought that they will live when he is dead. He already feels like a ghost. The author of the *Imitation of Christ*, he says, was content with anonymity because he believed in eternal life, but we, who lack faith, must pursue the shadow of immortality, even though we are aware of its illusoriness and continue to crave "substantial immortality, not a miserable deception". The narrator concludes by saying that if he were God he would condemn Don Martin to be forever locked up within his own statue. Fame would be his prison. But Don Martin's arguments are the same ones that Unamuno advances as his own in other places. He writes here against his own need for phantasmal glory.

Similar attitudes are found in stories and articles written at this time and even some years later. In "El maestro de Carrasqueda" (1903, IX, 182-7), an old schoolteacher says he is satisfied with being an anonymous influence in his village; what he has given the townspeople means more to him than achieving renown in the outside world. "Would you rather have your name cross the Pyrenees . . . or have your soul spill silently throughout Spain?" In an article published in 1915 Unamuno chides a young acquaintance for being more concerned with his name than with his soul, for not realizing that when a writer has enriched others, no matter how slightly, with a new idea, or even with a new metaphor or wish or illusion, he has saved his soul "in his people, in humanity" though his name may be forgotten (XI, 960).

But the attack on fame is less common than its contrary. From 1900 onwards Unamuno showed a markedly uncritical interest in the subject. In letters to his friend Ilundain he often spoke of the need to "make a name"; "one must preach ambition."[15] In 1901 he mentioned plans for a book on Herostratism,[16] and the next year he wrote that he did not know whether or not his own Herostratism, as well as his "mad, inextinguishable longing for individual perpetuation", were signs of illness; in any case, he was not looking for a cure. "My destiny as a man is to be a writer so that when I am gone, my works might remain."[17]

The endorsement of ambition, however, is frequently enmeshed in a tangle of parallel proposals, alternate ideas and counter-arguments and phrased in so round-about a way that it seems as if he were talking about something else. Sometimes the apparent subject has very little to do with fame, yet the essay can be fully understood only in the light of this hidden obsession. Unamuno often obscured his real aims, even when he revealed the conflict between them and his declared aspirations. This is the case in two of his most well-known essays, "¡Adentro!" ("Inwards!" III, 418-427) and "¡Plenitud de plenitudes y todo plenitud!" ("Plenitude of Plenitudes and All is Plenitude!" III, 753-70).

The first, published in 1900, is generally cited as one of the earliest documents of Unamuno's supposedly existentialist thought. In the passages that form the basis for this interpretation, he describes human life as a process that unfolds in time and he admonishes against living by predetermined and unexamined standards ("Do not have a plan! You are not a building!"). Since life creates

[15] Diego Catalán, "Tres Unamunos", pp. 67-8, note 91.
[16] Hernán Benítez, *El drama religioso de Unamuno* (Buenos Aires: Universidad de Buenos Aires, 1949), p. 344.
[17] Diego Catalán, "Tres Unamunos".

its own design as it evolves, one's finished personality is at the end and not the beginning of life; "only at death are you completed." "You discover yourself as you act." "As you change, let the ideal you make of yourself change." Such statements sound almost like anticipations of Ortega y Gasset's writings in the late nineteen twenties and thirties : man is the reality that cannot be fixed and defined because he has no "nature" but only a history; he creates his being in a dialectical series of choices and actions. The key formula of "¡Adentro !" – "My center is within myself !" – is taken as a summary expression of the inventive enterprise through which man makes himself, as one critic put it, "from within, but outside"; the argument is that "in opposition to any kind of essentialism, Unamuno here conceives life as a becoming, an appearing in time whose end is death".[18]

This interpretation runs into difficulty with other passages where Unamuno seems to return to his previous concept of an inner self unblemished by experience, though such passages are rich in ambiguity. He speaks of a person's eternal essence or depth ("fondo eterno") which is presumably established prior to its development in the world. "Your life is before your own consciousness a continual revelation in time of your eternity, the development of your symbol." Unamuno says that one should ignore the opinions of others and not bind the eternal essence, which unrolls in time, to its fugitive reflection. "Live for the day, in the waves of time, but anchored on your bed-rock, in the sea of eternity." Clearly, he is trying to tie together two incompatible ideas by making one the source of the other. But if temporal existence is the gradual revelation of an eternal design, how can he affirm the primacy of action and transformation ("as you change, let the ideal you make of yourself change")? The imagery of depths and surfaces recalls *En torno al casticismo*, and the conceptual mixture is very similar to the notion of the "daily eternal".[19]

If we consider the context and purpose of the essay, we can find a meaningful system in these ambiguities. "¡Adentro !" is written in the form of a letter to an unnamed author-friend who is evidently much distressed by his lack of success, and it begins with an impassioned plea for ambition. Unamuno assures his correspondent that his discouragement is both temporary and beneficial because the awareness of our "radical nothingness" is precisely what drives us "to aspire to be everything". He should strive for glory, for the heights, for the inaccessible; he must look beyond the Spanish public to a universal one, ignoring the reactions of neighbors and compatriots and taking himself as the sole guide of conduct. In proposing the motto "my center is within myself", Unamuno is not so much suggesting a program of self-invention as a defense against the judgments of others. All the letter's references to the inner world must be seen as reactions to the consequences of the literary ambition that Unamuno is recom-

[18] Carlos Blanco Aguinaga, "De Nicodemo a Don Quijote", in *Spanish Thought and Letters in the Twentieth Century*, p. 89.

[19] François Meyer says that in this essay "the relation of the eternal and the temporal is not . . . that of two planes of being, but that of two contradictory dimensions necessarily united in their very contradiction" (*La ontología de Miguel de Unamuno*, trans. C. Goicoechea, Madrid: Gredos, 1962, p. 58). Yet in discussing Pachico in *Paz en la guerra*, he had described the concept of "intrahistoria" as an escape from the anguish of being in time (p. 50).

mending so energetically. When the need for a public exposes him to scrutiny, he repudiates responsibility to anyone but himself.

The correspondent had evidently complained about his failure to make his mark upon the world; he has no followers and has not affected the history of ideas or the course of culture. Unamuno counsels his friend to aim at impressing a universal public (or even a single individual); then, reversing himself, he advises him to turn his back on the public in order to find the true self within. He would alternately court his readers and scorn them. The existentialist affirmation of the self achieved through acts and before others alternates with the fantasy of the inner world. Thus, although Unamuno says that man discovers himself in his acts, he shifts, in the very next sentence, to this picture of inwardness : "Go into the depths of your spirit and each day you will find new horizons, virgin lands, rivers of immaculate purity, skies never before seen, new stars and constellations." The inward voyage leads to an untouched, unseen landscape, pure and virginal because it is remote from any contact with the world.[20]

The person addressed in the letter is, of course, a mirror image of the author; Unamuno is dealing with his own divided feelings about his public. In a letter to Leopoldo Alas, he had confessed he held great hopes of winning recognition through the publication of this and two other essays and that an article by the influential critic would assure him more readers and the growth of "that wretched prestige we seek". And if his audience was disconcerted by the radical changes in his views in recent years, then all the more reason to oppose external consistency with internal continuity. Being a man of "goals and fixed intentions is nothing but being what the others imagine us to be; subjecting our reality to its appearance in their minds". When he says that one should never let one's past tyrannize over the future, he is preparing a get-away from his own previously published words. "Look only to the future . . . only the future is the realm of freedom." Indeed, all freedom is "ideal and only ideal . . . and inner". Those social reformers who try to make it "descend from the clouds and take form" are sadly misguided (he thus repudiates his earlier socialist stance.) In "¡Adentro!", as in "Nicodemo", freedom is in the wish and not the deed. A utopian liberty never put to the test of action is the mode of being of the inner self – total but imaginary autonomy.

In several passages Unamuno advises his friend to abandon the city and society and live in the peace of the countryside where he will not suffer from loneliness because "you yourself, in yourself, are society". The flight inwards is matched by the flight into Nature. The external natural landscape and the internal landscape of "immaculate purity" are interchangeable representations

---

[20] Blanco Aguinaga, who describes the refuge in nature as one of the essay's ambiguities, attributes it to the persistence of Unamuno's "contemplative" attitude; he believes he here abandons the thesis of "Nicodemo" about inner freedom and the timeless self in order to affirm the creation of the self in works ("De Nicodemo a Don Quijote", p. 90). But "¡Adentro!" includes both the thesis of "Nicodemo" and its contrary. As Blanco says, Unamuno accepted the "realist attitude" only reluctantly: he is quite correct in his suspicion that "Unamuno would never have accepted Ortega's claim that man has only History. This is the substance of his agony; its principle" (p. 99). See also Blanco's " 'Authenticity' and the Image", in *Unamuno, Creator and Creation*, ed. Barcia and Zeitlin (Berkeley, Los Angeles: University of California Press, 1967), pp. 48-71.

of the ideal of isolation and self-sufficiency. "¡Adentro!", for all its exhortations about committing and creating the self through works, is really one more version of Unamuno's recurrent dream of a self divinely independent and perpetually uncommitted. The quest for identity in the eyes of others intensifies the longing for the unseen and private self.

The pattern of "¡Adentro!" is anticipated in the Diary in the context of severe self-criticism. I have cited the passage where he says that with our conduct we fabricate a "poor copy" of ourselves; the entry is titled "Slavery" and is preceded by a description of his desire to see himself from without. "We are attentive only to the effect our words and acts produce on our fellow men" (176). It is the need for validating oneself in the eyes of others that enslaves us. Yet the alternative is perhaps "worse" because if we despise applause and seek only our own satisfaction, we are guilty of a "masturbatory pride" (175). Thus, although the search for the reflected image of the self leads into a ghostly world of imaginary bondage, the alternative is the lonely sin of onanism.[21]

In "Plenitud de plenitudes", the tension between the twin illusions of the self outside and the self within breaks at significant moments into a nihilistic dream of peace, showing us the other side of self-desire. The essay opens with the evocation of the Spirit of Dissolution that forever haunts man, nagging him with the futility of his efforts to win "name and prestige" when he has only a few days on the surface of the earth. Unamuno clearly enjoys reminding us that it has always been the poets, those enamored of glory, who have sung its vanity, recording for future generations their vision of the paltriness of human achievement. The old preacher's admonition is nonetheless dispiriting and Unamuno says we must oppose it with another entreaty – "plenitude of plenitude and all is plenitude!" In the rest of the essay he suggests various definitions of "plenitude" and several counter-arguments to Ecclesiastes.

To attain fullness of being, "seek your soul with the arms of your soul and embrace it and rub up against it and feel how substantial and warm it is". Those people who have no sense of their own psychical presence, which Unamuno calls "spiritual kinesthesia", and who do not "feel the weight of their own soul nor its contact", are nothing but "automata" without reflexive consciousness. For Unamuno consciousness does not mean simply self-awareness but belief in or the desire for personal immortality: the man who accepts mortality (and the vanity of worldly efforts) "does not have full possession of himself, he lacks the intuition of his own substantiality". Unamuno shifts, however, from the identification of substance with the desire for immortality to its identification with the pursuit of fame ("if, in search of plenitude, I go after prepotency and the conquest of renown . . ."). Throughout the essay he talks sometimes about immortality and sometimes about its "shadow" and we can never be sure which is being defined as "substance". Renown is won in the outside

---

[21] Antonio Machado, who shared so many of Unamuno's concerns but who wrote about them in a much lighter and more self-mocking tone, claimed that "Onan sometimes knows a great deal which Don Juan knows nothing about" ("Aunque a veces sabe Onán/mucho que ignora Don Juan"; these lines are attributed to Abel Martín, one of Machado's pseudonymous alter-egos; *Abel Martín* in *Poesías completas*, Madrid: Austral, 1940, p. 231); Onan at least acknowledges the reflexive nature of his passion.

world, in the admiration of others. Yet Unamuno refers to the concrete self that manifests itself in fame as an entirely private phenomenon whose existence is immediately and inwardly perceived.

The most significant contradiction is that seeking fame and craving immortality are offered as evidence of spiritual weight when Unamuno's own language shows instead that they are the result of the experience of insufficiency and emptiness. When he speaks of "the longing to extend oneself in space and time" we remember what he said in "¡Adentro!" about how the feeling of our "radical nothingness" makes us want to be everything and conclude that this longing must spring from a similar sense of "nothingness". Yet that is what Unamuno calls substance. The desire for substance is thus made proof of its possession. What is implied, though not explicity stated, and the indirection is surprising in view of Unamuno's fondness for paradoxes, is that plenitude is ontological hunger – fullness of being is the consciousness of emptiness. Either he is not fully aware of the conceptual fusion or he does not want the reader to be too aware of it.[22]

At this point, without any transition, there appears a passage describing a mystical union of consciousness and the world in which expansive striving is replaced by beatific peace and quietude. Evidently the unavowed equation between emptiness and fullness allows him to present first the one and then the other experience of "substantiality" – first longing, then fulfillment – without acknowledging any reversal in thought. For people of spiritual sensitivity, the "visual, sonorous, and tactile crust of the world" breaks open and the "substance of things splits the crust of the soul" so that the two penetrate and mingle. "The world descends and settles into the entrails of their souls." This union is the "other world . . . the substance of the one we see, hear, and touch . . . a mysterious and sacred world where nothing passes and all endures".[23] The conscious effort to augment the self and absorb the world turns into communion and stasis. One might think that the second is either a repudiation of the first or its reward, but actually it is neither, because Unamuno is attempting – as he does repeatedly throughout the essay – to effect in images and words a coalescence of contrary feelings. He desperately wants to believe that neediness is abundance and that self-seeking is communion. So he imagines that desire can bridge the gap between the real and the ideal; he always said, after all, that wanting to believe is the same as believing – "What basis is there for faith in immortality? . . . the fact that I want it!"

[22] The critics who have observed that the notion of substance alternates with that of the void, associate the first with the "contemplative" Unamuno and the second with the "agonist". Paul Olson says that "despite the apparent polarity of these two attitudes toward interiority, it is clear that in purely structural terms, they are virtually identical. In the *Recuerdos* Unamuno tells us that . . . he had learned from Balmes of Hegel's concept of the identity of pure being and pure nothingness" ("The Novelistic *Logos* in Unamuno's *Amor y pedagogía*", *MLN*, 84 (1969) p. 263). But Unamuno's fusion of being and nothingness has nothing to do with Hegel for the simple reason that it is not explicit and probably not even conscious.

[23] Very similar words are used in describing the world of *intrahistoria* in *En torno al casticismo* (III, 184-87) and, in *San Manuel Bueno, mártir*, the one created by literary fiction (XVI, p. 628).

The ecstatic vision of fulfilment and repose vanishes as abruptly as it appeared; the text returns to the obsessive need for perpetuation and to its inevitable concomitant – the fantasy of reunion with an inner self. The person who covets fame needs the others and yet he does not want to admit that dependence; he is always vulnerable, always open to the sting of rejection – and so he turns inwards. Plenitude can be achieved by "embracing the soul with the arms of the soul and feeling its spiritual concreteness in spite of the mockery, rancor, contempt, envy or indifference of others". *They* are always there, and to get away from them he takes refuge in the inner world. But he cannot give up his endeavors to seduce them and win their approval. Wanting to "leave a name" is a "natural flowering of the faith in one's own existence",[24] and that faith makes us try to impose ourselves on the imaginations and memories of others. People who are not interested in being noticed, he says, are deficient in spiritual vitality.

The rest of the essay deals with those stunted creatures who harp on the vanity of glory and regard this life as chimerical and illusory. Yet even here Unamuno is ambivalent and equivocal for, while he finds the vision of life as a dream dreadful yet profound in Calderón and Shakespeare, he has nothing but scorn for Renan, whom he calls the modern exponent of that "hypnotic sense of the world and of life" which makes one regard everything as sheer spectacle. Such "estheticism" (alway a negative term in Unamuno) is a "philosophy of somnambulists who do not feel their own spiritual weight". Against that philosophy Unamuno affirms that nothing passes without leaving a trace of itself – "everything will be remembered".

"La locura del Dr. Montarco" ("The Madness of Dr. M.", III, 685-700) was written the same year as "Plenitud". The story's protagonist, whose situation is very similar to Unamuno's, is a physician in a provincial city who takes to writing odd, humorous stories. Though he is a conscientious doctor, his patients begin to feel uneasy about his professional qualifications and little by little stop consulting him. As if in response to this reception, the stories become somewhat aggressive, full of thinly veiled ironic attacks on the readers : Montarco finds himself engaged in a kind of battle with the town, people accuse him of pride while he complains about their stupidity and narrowmindedness. When the narrator talks about this with Montarco he discovers that the doctor, so simple and unassuming in his everyday life, is driven by an all-consuming pride and a compulsive need to affirm his superiority. He speaks of having to dominate others as if his life depended on it : "the man who tries to overcome and master others is only trying to save himself." Yet for Montarco mastery is not a matter of controlling the actions of others but only of impressing them – for him domination means fame. Its pursuit involves one in an aggressive relation with all others who are regarded either as potential public or potential rivals; one can enlarge one's own image only by "sinking the name of others into oblivion".

---

[24] A few years later Unamuno argued that doubt in one's existence, not faith, is the sign of genuine existence (1915, X, p. 318); in "Una entrevista con Augusto Pérez" (same year) he says that "the most liberating thing about art is that it makes one doubt that one exists . . . a man who is very convinced of his own concrete reality is a terrible thing" (X, p. 335).

Montarco compares men's competitive battle for fame with flies scrambling in a water bottle, killing each other in order to stay afloat. "The struggle for fame is a thousand times more terrible than the struggle for bread." Men's works are always motivated more by the "instinct of invasion" than by that of survival. "We strive not to maintain ourselves but to be more, to be everything". Satan tempts us with an "appetite for divinity" ("you will be like gods") but if we do not yield we will end up being nothing. "All or nothing!"

Montarco explains his enmity towards his competitors but not his equally combative behavior towards his public. In "¡Adentro!" and "Plenitud" we saw the vulnerability of the person who needs to be noticed. It is evident here too: Montarco vilifies the readers he so ardently desires to impress because he sees, but does not admit, that the domination he craves is really subjection – thus the hostility to both rivals and public, the "instinct of invasion", and the need constantly to attack. When his verbal aggression becomes alarming, he is put in a madhouse where he spends his time re-reading the *Quijote* and preaching to his visitors about the quixotic nobility of fame-seeking: if God created the world for his greater glory, do we not have to emulate Him? Should we be less than God? The narrator obviously thinks that much of what the doctor says shows great good sense. The director of the asylum agrees, for perhaps this unquenchable thirst for immortality is "the revelation of another world which supports and sustains ours". The ravings of the mad might be the spirit's frantic leaps to reach that other world; madmen may be estranged from ordinary reality but they are attuned to a higher one. In an essay written the same year ("Sobre la filosofía española") Unamuno spoke of how the instinct of perpetuation, the hunger for greatness, discloses the other world that exists beyond or within the apparent one. In all of Unamuno's writings, the "other world" refers to that magical place where "nothing passes and all endures" and where the pain of isolation and rancor disappear in the peace of reconciliation. The antics of the mad certainly do point to the ideal of reunion and integration, though not in the way that Unamuno intends – not as the secret content of their raving but as its perfect antithesis.

To run continually after one's image in the mind of others is, for Unamuno, the archetypal heroic enterprise and Don Quijote the most exalted model of the hero. In *La vida de Don Quijote y Sancho* (1905, IV, 65-383), Unamuno's encomium of earthly glory, he says that the root of the "divine" quixotic madness is the fear of death: we must try to expand our personality in space and prolong it in time or else we cease to exist. "At bottom, vainglory is nothing but the terror of nothingness, a thousand times more dreadful than hell itself." Although he occasionally reverts to the distinction between immortality and its "shadow", he tends in this book, as he had in "Montarco", to confound the two. The choice is "God or oblivion" because we must see to it that God does not forget us. What is needed to confirm one's sense of existence is the consciousness of another – either God or man ("We must aspire to be famous and immortal"). The book ends with the author asking Don Quixote to intercede in his favor so that Dulcinea can lead him by the hand to "the immortality of name and of fame". Such is the nature of heroism.

But the hero, he tells us, is seen only from the outside and therefore, ironically, always misunderstood and doomed to solitude. The praise of quixotism in this book goes hand in hand with a sustained and bitter invective against the insensitivity and stupidity of the hero's – and Unamuno's – public. Characteristically the condemnation of the others is worked into the theory of public and private selves through which Unamuno repeatedly tried to convince himself of a hidden integrity behind the implications of words and acts. The hero sees himself from within, as he wants to be; the others see him as he is. "You should not worry about what you are; the cardinal thing is what you want to be. The one you are is nothing but an ephemeral and perishable thing . . . that the earth will swallow up one day; the self you want to be is your idea in God . . . the divine idea of which you are a manifestation in time and space."

This is essentially the same argument as that of "Nicodemo" but its subsequent development reverses some of the central points made there. In the earlier essay we never really know what the inner desire is like; in fact, its secret nature is its greatest attraction. Here Unamuno gives the inner intention a specific quality and a name – ambition. Adam's "happy fault", he says, was wanting to be God's equal and each man can be redeemed by imitating that arrogant wish; the true self, one's idea in God, is the self that lusts for fame. This is a most peculiar and significant inversion and it is worth noting the missing step that Unamuno has so carefully obscured. What he does not say, either in this book or in the many other writings devoted to the topic – but what is everywhere obvious – is that the thirst for glory puts one at the mercy of the public. The threat to personal autonomy and the consequent defensive reactions – aggression towards others and the theory of the private untouchable self – increase in proportion to the need for fame. So successful is he in suppressing the consciousness of this tie that he manages in this book (and in *Del sentimiento trágico de la vida*) to present a concept of the inner self that totally belies its real origin : he situates it not in the landscape of immaculate inner purity, but in the outer world where reputations are won and lost in competition with others. Emptiness is fullness, the inner self is the outer one. Unamuno cannot acknowledge this fusion because he needs the dualistic scheme to preserve the illusion of autonomy and freedom. So he spins rapidly from one position to the other, developing both in parallel but unconnected arguments and hoping thereby to create the appearance of independence and control in the very circumstances in which it cannot exist – in a life dedicated to the creation of one's image in the minds of others.

Underlying both the ideal of inwardness and the obsession with fame is the same alienating illusion of a consistent self, solid and immutable as an object and magically impervious to the contingencies of experience or the demands of others. Both arise out of the same fear of insubstantiality that accompanies the ideal of the substantial ego. Since the two ideas are so intimately connected, it is not surprising that they continually supplant each other. Walled up in the inner fortress, he suffers from loneliness and despair; with the external world shut out, he can perceive only his "radical nothingness". Since he does not partake of life, he hungers and thirsts for "divinity" and longs "to be more, to be everything". When he tries to conquer others and win earthly renown, he cannot help but feel his ultimate subjection. He retreats again. The closer he comes in his imagination to one goal, the more destructive it appears and the more urgent the need to escape. The final strategy is total evasiveness. He is constantly on the run.

II

Isolation vs. Action

Invasion and retreat are the natural maneuvers of what his readers have come to see as the "agonic" Unamuno who insistently proclaimed a "battlefield morality". The references to the "other world" suggest, however, another mode of relating to people and to external reality in general. The warrior's sense of isolation must be acute, so at moments he yearns for the company of others and the fraternal embrace of the world. But such fraternization always appeared extremely hazardous to Unamuno because it threatened to dissolve his individual identity. He often expressed his horror of mystical states in which the soul merges with God or with the All. It must have seemed to him that as soon as he gave up his defensive or offensive posture, the world would flood in on him, drowning the cherished inner substance. He had to fight to guard his personal frontiers, the boundary line between himself and the menacing fullness outside him. In "Plenitud" he said he was terrified by the "delight in one's own dissolution". He was always suspicious of the lulling and melting effects of music. Yet there are many times when the danger is transformed into an alluring temptation and he dreams of losing himself in unconsciousness, sleep, eternity – or in nature which offers "a soft bath of resigned abandon", where one is "freed from the obsession of life".[1] Carlos Blanco Aguinaga has given us an exhaustive study of Unamuno's "contemplative" inclination in its several thematic variations – the mother, the wife (usually the woman who is mother to her husband), the symbolic imagery of water (sea, lake, rain), the "lap" of nature, etc. – and in its different emotional colorings, from the positive vision of union with God to the despairing acceptance of nothingness into which Unamuno sometimes sinks from exhaustion.[2] There is no need to repeat Blanco's careful survey, but I would like to examine the way the desire for mystical fusion appears – often at the expense of coherence – in the works considered typically "agonic". It should also become clear that the dissolution of the self is at times envisioned as a merging with others, as when Unamuno writes about a "distant reign of the spirit" when the contents of each individual soul will pour out and the "sentiments, longings, and most inward feelings and hidden thoughts" will "ooze out . . . and congeal in a single spiritual mist, a common soul, in which float the shells of our spirits" ("A lo que salga", 1904, III, p. 798).

Blanco Aguinaga sees the "contemplative" and the "agonistic" as two modes of being which alternate but do not conflict and he attributes the internal division to the fact that the "tragic fate" of Unamuno, "candid, mystical, and

[1] "El perfecto pescador de caña. Después de leer a Walton" ("The Compleat Angler. On Reading Walton", 1904, III, pp. 771-88).
[2] *El Unamuno contemplativo.*

tender" by nature, was to have lost his faith (p. 290). Other critics who have commented on Unamuno's contradictory desires have, as we saw, also explained them in terms of two Unamunos, the religious believer and the public doubter, characterizing the first as the original or childhood self and the other as the one created through the development of his thought and through his public posturing.[3] The two-self theory was, as I have said, Unamuno's own. But since it does not reveal the tie between the contrary aims it cannot account for the inevitability of self-reversal.[4] The dynamics of internal conflict are hardened into stable and consistent entities that for unknown reasons are apt to replace each other.

So far we have seen the veerings between the fantasy of the inner self and the equally illusory image of the external one. This oscillation is, as I have said, enclosed within and complicated by another pattern which shifts between the hopeless grasping at his own self and the nostalgic yearning for engulfment. The experience of estrangement that necessarily accompanies the frenetic pursuit of inward substance or outward reflection makes him long for union; yet the dread of being swallowed or of losing the boundaries of the ego in mystical transport pushes a retreat into the confines of his isolated and embattled self. His greatest terror thus suddenly becomes his fondest desire.

Because Unamuno did not see the connection between the wish for perfect autonomy and the yearning for absorption, his description of either one leads into an equivocal tangle where contraries cross and mingle. The fundamental unity of his opposing desires accounts for many of the contradictions between various essays. Thus in "Soledad" (1905, III, 881-903) Unamuno recommends seclusion whereas he often said that such a state reveals only the phantom of one's self; the true personality is manifested in society. Crucial contradictions, as we have seen, also occur within a single essay ("¡Adentro!", for instance, makes irreconcilable assertions about solitude). "Soledad" is an excellent example of the effect of the reversibility of aims on the structure of Unamuno's prose. The essay appears to be a defense of solitude but the argument alters its course so frequently and disconcertingly that the reader must search for another argument, hidden, fragmented, and only intermittently discernible, that lies beneath – and explains – the inconsistencies of the surface text. Unamuno's language points to a deeper language and his "false consciousness" bespeaks the true nature of his desires. Obfuscation can be a form of revelation.

I shall describe the progression of the essay which, from the very first, shows

---

[3] See Introduction, note 21.

[4] I do not think that one can find in these mutually negating efforts the dialectical pattern that Blanco Aguinaga and Paul Olson propose in their recent works. There is a difference between dialectics and oscillations that go nowhere. Unamuno's profoundly irrational and "idealistic dialectic", which stops at antithesis (at what Unamuno called *agonía*), cannot be identified with Hegelian dialectic. Elías Díaz points out that under the apparent dynamism of struggle and the clash of contradictions, there is "immobility and conservatism". We have not a dialectic but a "mere esthetics of contradiction for contradiction's sake" (op. cit., p. 168). In the realm of social thought, this "arbitrary and passionate method, this irrational dialectic", means a lack of understanding and connection with concrete reality, though one could easily invert the terms and see Unamuno's irrationality as a response to and a consequence of his break with reality (p. 173).

how his notion of solitude inclines towards solipsism and necessitates the conversion of other persons into phantasmal projections. It begins :

> If I am so eager to get away from him it is . . . because I love him so much. I flee from him, seeking him. When I have him next to me, and see his look and hear his words, I wish I could extinguish his glance and make him mute forever; but then, when I am away from him and alone with myself, I see two little lights emerging from the murky depths of my consciousness, blinking like twin stars in the bottomless night, and I hear in my silence remote and faint sounds that seem to come from the infinite and never quite reach me. They are his eyes and his words; his eyes purified by absence and distance, his words purified by silence. And that is why I flee from him in order to find him, and why I avoid him because I love him.
>
> Love, when it is pure and noble, grows with distance. The farther his body is from me, the closer his soul. He left me his soul in a few words, in a glance, and already he lives, and grows and develops in me.

The other is Unamuno's image of him, his voice is the one Unamuno gives him, his thoughts and words the ones Unamuno imagines him to have. A docile figment of the author's imagination, he has no more autonomous existence than the characters of a novel. It is not surprising that Unamuno persistently equated real people with fictitious characters, for he finds them all inside himself : "I seek . . . within my soul the company of people" because "only solitude can melt away the thick layer of formality that separates us from each other; only in solitude can we find ourselves", and in so doing, find "all of our brothers in solitude". The best way to get to know someone is to avoid him.

Unamuno says that too often relations with people in the world are based on sham and deception, with men hiding their real thoughts and feelings behind "the thick crust of convention that separates us from others and from God". He himself must feel guilty of duplicity because he yearns for the "redeeming hymn of confession that can be sung only in solitude where we have no secrets from God". He regards even confession as a solitary thing, a secret transmitted to God and jealously guarded from men. Seeing very little possibility of honest dealings with others, he opts for radical seclusion.

His own sense of isolation is striking. When he says that the only true dialogue is "the one you have with yourself" and that what usually pass as such are really only "intersecting monologues" (Unamuno called some of his essays "monodialogues") he gives the impression of total incommunicability. Yet, not wanting to make an explicit defense of solipsism, he argues that when we are alone we are able to touch our common human core, which he defines as the anguished preoccupation with immortality ("what will become of my consciousness, of yours, and of his, and of everyone's when each one of us dies?"). This is, however, an unusual bond because it requires that we keep away from our neighbor the better to ruminate on individual fate.

For all his praise of solitude, we sense an intense loneliness; to overcome it he imagines a wonderful kind of community that poses none of the problems of real people and real relationships – the self with its own projections and fantasies. "If you knew what I owe to my sweet solitude . . . If you knew how the affection I have for you has grown!" This tender feeling is menaced by the intrusion of the flesh-and-blood friend : "when you talk, your voice crashes in my ears and breaks the train of my own thoughts : your figure interposes itself between my eyes and the familiar shapes on which they rest." The bond of solitude is strictly internal; he includes all otherness within himself. The aim is omnipotence and his undeclared wish is to be the creator of himself and of others. In the play *Soledad* (1921) the protagonist, a playwright, says he wants to be "author, actor, and public . . . and God . . . Father, Son, and Holy Ghost. And one true God. I myself" (XII, p. 613). Creation would be a kind of self-impregnation; in an article called "The Fecundity of Isolation" he wrote that the most intimate and fertile truth a solitary person can discover is within himself; thus Walt Whitman "put himself in contact with himself . . . embraced himself and discovered his soul and in it, the soul of everyone else" (IX, 814-15).

The need for autonomy evokes, as we have seen, the most contrary feelings about the writer's public. Responding to the accusation that he was dancing to the tune called by his audience ("you no longer belong to yourself but to them"), Unamuno says that although they think he jumps and gyrates in time to their clapping, it is really the other way around; he does not need others to show him the steps – "That is the advantage of dancing alone." The truly solitary person is the one who can dance in the middle of the public square before a large crowd but to a celestial music he alone, "by virtue of his solitude", can hear. He thus describes his need for the public (why else dance in the town square?) and his indifference to them. He would make his disdain itself a public performance.

No sooner does he proclaim his total freedom than he begins to long for company; he complains that people are impenetrable, that they can communicate in only the most superficial way. He would like, he says, to shake them up and throw them against each other so that their crusts would break and souls would spill out to "mix, meld, and fuse with each other". Eager to get inside them, he speaks of "crashing against people . . . straight on . . . and splitting them down the middle" (and for this, the best preparation is solitude). His language preserves the hostility of the previous phase; so rapid is the shift from the ideal of perfect autonomy to the ideal of communion, that love and hate, dependence and indifference, are confused in the vocabulary of combat. Although he is the one who wanted freedom, he now describes isolation as a condition imposed upon him against his will. He must speak from personal experience (experiences I shall discuss later) when he refers to those people who think that they are the only living creatures in the world and that others are empty shells "that by a strange magic move, speak, and act as if they were really alive". Such a notion might take one to the edge of madness, as in the case of an acquaintance who sometimes imagined that he was completely different from what he knew he was : when he thought he was engaging in friendly conversation it occurred to him that he might really be insulting the other person; when he walked down the street in a dignified way, he might really be jumping about and acting the fool so that those who passed by seeming not to notice him, were really laughing at him. This man ended up in the insane asylum, but Unamuno says that anyone who "speaks with his heart in his hand" is apt to feel this way; dissociation would seem to be the inevitable result of sincerity. An explanation more plausible than Unamuno's would be that such a schizophrenic break is the consequence of the attempt to achieve an impossible autonomy by putting oneself beyond others and beyond the world. Separating the "dirty crust born of the flesh, of the world" from the pure transcendent self, lays the groundwork for the hallucinatory experience of the body as an alien being with a life of its own : it could very well do all kinds of surprising things and mock every pretense of control; it might very well do just the opposite of what the real self wills. At the extreme of solitude, the concrete world of objects and bodies turns into sheer illusion.

But the barren experience of incommunicability has nothing to do, in Unamuno's mind, with the fact that he shuns the presence of others; quite the contrary, he says the others are the spiritual crustaceans whose hard shells conceal an inner emptiness. People accuse him of confiding in everyone, but that is only because he considers all men his brothers. The "others", the "crustaceans", confide in no one because they have nothing to confide; their reserve is simply emptiness; "and all this produces an enormous feeling of loneliness". So he will cherish and cultivate his own solitude, regretting only that he cannot protect himself with "real" isolation as well; he would like to retreat to the desert, not out of disdain for others, he assures us, but only in order to instruct, for the man who insults the masses is really paying homage to each individual who composes it.

Then, breaking away suddenly from this strange knot of anger and altruistic concern, he returns to the theme of confession. He imagines a future age of the spirit when the great social institution will be public confession. There will be no secrets and no one will need be ashamed of impure desires or uncharitable thoughts. When all souls are naked, Unamuno says, men will discover that they are much better than they thought they were and will pity and pardon themselves and others. Solitude will disappear because men will accept themselves and resign themselves to imperfection. Unamuno shows that the way to be released from moral exile is to reveal one's fallibility, not just to God but to ordinary mortals.

But this insight is a momentary achievement in the essay because he quickly reverts to the alluring image of uniqueness, once again setting up the figure of "the great solitary man" as model and guide. The possibility of contact with others gives way to this visionary image of inner wealth. "The solitary man has an entire society within him; he is legion . . . the man of genius . . . is a multitude." His hope for communication and confession yields to a dream of fusion and the fantasy of total self-sufficiency. That fantasy, with which the essay closes, reconciles contrary needs; just as the solitary man embraces imaginary companions in the privacy of an inner world, the man of genius feels that he contains within himself all others. Since we have seen that such self-sufficiency easily leads to total estrangement, the tension between opposites that characterizes the entire essay is never resolved. Thus when Unamuno concludes that the solitary man thinks aloud and says what others dare think only in secret, we cannot be sure if he is betraying pride or an ironic and self-conscious humility. The theme, he tells us finally, is inexhaustible. The essay can never end. Surely inexhaustible is the author himself who perpetually twists and turns between isolation and union, frenzy and reason.

*   *   *

A few pages in "Soledad" point to those intermissions in Unamuno's personal drama when, stepping out of his roles as aggressor or defender, he describes a truce that would permit the rebuilding of all that is destroyed by the disasters of war. He proposes a mode of being that at once liberates the self and permits communication. Yet the truce is always precarious and the hard-won insight tends all too easily to slide back into loneliness and despair.

The way out of the self and into the world is through action. As I have said, Unamuno often returned to certain of his socialist views; during the period 1895-1905 he frequently emphasized the significance of the objective import of words and deeds. We have seen that in those passages where he stressed the value of action, he repudiated the theory of a special inner path to self-know-ledge. Man is the offspring of his works and in them he comes to know himself. Unamuno continues to affirm this in later works even when, as in *La vida de Don Quijote y Sancho*, he makes a desperate effort to turn the affirmation into a definition of its opposite by saying that our works constitute our fame and create the image that others have of us.

That Unamuno was often enough quite conscious of this duality is evident in the Diary where he described the tension between the active life – a life dedi-cated to interests and needs that extend beyond the boundaries of the self – and what he called the "spiritual masturbation" of inner suffering. But this awareness only heightens the desire for purity and clarity; the effort to overcome his divided feelings and contradictory ideas sets consciousness against itself, leading him ever deeper into a tangle of disguised motives and denied wishes. Attitudes and feelings keep turning into their opposites, mocking his anxious reach for sincerity and truthfulness. Thus he refers to his anonymous contri-butions to *La Lucha de Clases* as a "constant campaign for an elevated, noble, charitable socialism, a campaign in which I did not think of myself", and, in the very next phrase ("I hid myself"), reveals that even thoughtless service for the cause of others can be a way of masking the self and seeking "sinful" isola-tion. And when he goes on to speak of that service in terms of abnegation, we realize that he comes perilously close to a humility that is nothing other than the public face of arrogance.

In the Diary Unamuno repeatedly asks that God grant him the grace of humility, that he "free him from himself". But because he tends to confound humility with self-negation ("in myself I am truly nothing", p. 147) and appears over-ready to accept suffering, one suspects the hidden presence of a self-exalting and dominating cruelty. "I do not want to will; I want to obey. Let them command me!" (219). He longs for humiliation and disgrace. "Humiliation, great humiliation! Humiliation in order to be humble! A crown of thorns, ridicule, a reed for a scepter, bloody mockery, and the grace, oh Lord, to endure them" (279-80). It is not really surprising to find the dream of punishment so

24

emotionally inflated or to discover that the dreamer identifies himself with none less than the divine victim. Immediately afterwards comes the abashed recognition of pride. "These notebooks themselves, are they not vanity? Why do I write them? ... Oh, that I would think not of myself and my glory, but only of yours, my Lord!" (281). He knows very well how highly he esteems his own suffering. He even manages to take pride in the very pridefulness he struggles against. "I tend to think that this inner pride ... is an elaborate and exquisite disease that only a few of us are allowed to suffer" (298). The underlying unity of arrogance and abnegation forms the dramatic nucleus of those fictions in which, as we shall see, Unamuno portrays the destructive complicity of master and slave.

Over and over in the Diary we see that the veerings between self-aggrandizement and self-torture are the alternations of a single lust for glory that is itself rooted in the experience of an overwhelming lack – nothingness – *la nada*. It is here for the first time that Unamuno formulates one of his solutions to the satanic demand for "all or nothing". "Only by making ourselves nothing can we become everything" (99). The plea for the grace of humility becomes more frequent in the later entries where it is combined with references to God's paternity; it is to God the Father that he yearns to submit. "If it is delicious to be heard by God ... it is even more delicious to sacrifice oneself to the will of God" (403-4). Yet he does not say much more about action or about charity. Somehow in the heightened eagerness for subjection and obedience, the saving grace of action is forgotten. In the late entries, Unamuno seems to abandon the real world for a purely private one, swept away by a passion for submission.

One of the essays during the years 1895-1905 stands out from all the others because, pointing up the deviousness of Unamuno's most characteristic ways of arguing, it repudiates both the wish for self-possession and the wish for annihilation; it is titled "On Pride" ("Sobre la soberbia", 1904, III, 806-20). He begins by observing that we always hate, or love, that which is most like us. "It is my envy , my pride, my petulance and greed that make me abhor the pride, envy, petulance, and greed of others." Hatred unites people and constitutes a bond as strong and durable as love. Indeed, Unamuno argues, it frequently rests on the support of love since the two feelings are by no means mutually exclusive. The intolerance we combat in others is then our own intolerance. Therefore people who are truly humble are never outraged or offended by the vanity of others. He says that pride has always been condemned in the spirit of pride itself. Those who are "humble by profession" must take special care that their humility does not turn into its opposite for the most sophisticated pride is that of the person who humbles himself in order to be exalted.

Unamuno describes the various guises of arrogance. There is the person who seeks to be praised for his selflessness. The monk in his cell who strives for humility and purity finds within himself the very evil from which he flees. Unamuno often said that people who live in cloisters are the ones most tempted by wordly sins. And the greatest temptation is the passion of pride.

From this Unamuno concludes that committing a sinful act "purifies us from the terrible desire that was eating away at our hearts" (we are reminded of Nietzsche, though Unamuno never mentions him when their views are most similar).[5] The murderer, Unamuno claims, begins to feel compassion and even love as soon as his crime has freed him from hate. Worse than murder is "nourishing one's sensibility with hate, a life corroded by evil desires." Feelings that are contained poison the blood and corrupt the spirit. One becomes evil by swallowing one's own venom. So we must distinguish between doing good and being good, for "although one knows a tree by its fruits . . . good acts spring from good souls". It is one thing to do evil and another to be evil. There are many people, says Unamuno, who die without ever having performed a single bad act and who, nevertheless, have never cherished a single good wish, people who secretly delight in the evil they are not capable of doing. Others, who continually molest those around them and even hurt them, die without ever having felt malice towards anyone.

Rancor, says Unamuno, is the inescapable consequence of an external discipline that prohibits any show of violence. It is no good confessing evil deeds if we guard in our hearts the secret of evil thoughts. Such thoughts blossom into demoniacal creeds, such as the Christian belief in hell, which Unamuno describes with ironic relish. Thus the ideal of holiness breeds monstrous passions and the law itself creates sin. Or we might extend Unamuno's argument and say that the original sin – the desire to be God's equal – gives rise to all moral codes. Unamuno writes that we must follow not the strictures of an externally applied law but the living rule which he calls the law of sincerity that brings into accord emotions and acts and makes our deeds "the offspring of our sentiments and our words the revelation of our thought". In this essay Unamuno tries to formulate a morality beyond isolationist conceptions of good and evil, beyond impossible standards that condemn the person who would be God to the burden of guilt and defeat. The ideal of saintliness (as we see in the Diary) leads only to the continuous torment of self-castigation, and the pain increases in direct proportion to the shameful realization that it is itself one more devious claim to superiority. Unamuno knew quite well that between all and nothing there is something else after all –imperfection, fallibility and error – and also the community of men.

Here he argues that all disguises must be dropped. One should not hide inner pride behind a studied humility that is no humility at all; one might as well confess feelings of superiority and let others think one vain. Indeed, the truest humility would be allowing others to believe that one is arrogant – even desiring that they think that. At this point, however, Unamuno approaches the abso-

[5] Unamuno often attacked the man he called "poor Nietzsche", the man who "sick in body and spirit all his life, dreamed of what he was not, of what he could not be" (IX, p. 78), a weak man who "invented the sophistry of strength" (IV, p. 850). He also said, however, that "one can still sympathize with Nietzsche's soul even while abominating his teachings" (IV, p. 851). Not surprisingly, he saw in him a kind of mirror image, "*ecce homo* – and it is so painful to hear oneself" (VIII, p. 1102), and an envy of Christ that was, nevertheless, "tragic and grandiose" (V, p. 266). The Basque journalist Salaverría said Unamuno was envious of Nietzsche, and Paul Ilie has pointed out that "the insistence on certain features of Nietzsche's profile is striking because of their resemblance to the Spaniard himself" (*Unamuno, an Existential View of Self and Society*, Madison: University of Wisconsin, 1967, p. 130; see all of Part Two, "Nietzschean Categories", pp. 119-94). This, of course, is precisely what Unamuno tells us at the beginning of "On Pride" – "we only hate, and only love, that which is like us".

lutist frame of reference that would see Judas as the true Christ. But he pulls himself up short; no, true humility is not worrying about what opinion others may have. All affectations are wrong; even pride frequently manifests itself in its own falsification because people try to disarm criticism through confession. Unamuno turns the admission of pride into an exoneration. We might add that such an admission is at least a way of keeping a jump ahead of one's judges.

Yet Unamuno recognizes that excessive devotion to self-scrutiny and self-punishment can become the source of new ills. "This worrying of conscience over itself is life's greatest affliction." Continual rumination corrodes the "spiritual stomach" so that contemplative and ruminating souls end by digesting themselves, "dissolving themselves in the juice of their own scruples and cavils". The soul becomes, Unamuno says, satanic, its own enemy.

The cure for this destructive examination is action. "Let us act, for pride that acts is redeemed and does not poison." Unamuno tells us that we should not torment ourselves with the agonies of self-discovery but try to learn only what we can do. Thus pride that moves from contemplation to action loses its poison and may even become a virtue – *virtus*, valor. He believes that pride which exposes itself to the judgments of others ceases to be evil. The greatest humility shows itself in works. Although the Christian mystics and ascetics have said that the greatest act of humility was the incarnation and sacrifice of the Son of God, Unamuno argues that "the very act of creation . . . was an act of supreme humility" because, in making the world, God offered it to the judgment and censure of his creatures. All doing, he concludes, is humble, whereas inaction and passivity are often the masks of arrogance.

Against the dark secrets of self-contained passions, Unamuno preaches purification through works and through public confession. In "A lo que salga" which was written a few months earlier, Unamuno also speaks of confession, but there it is a means of attaining mystical communion and dissolving the self "in a single spiritual mist, a common soul". That the pain of finiteness and individuality is not accepted is evident in his shift from the admission of weakness and delusion to the imagined peace of personal disintegration. What he is after is not really contact and connection, but merging and non-differentiation. Confession remains in the realm of the imaginary. In this essay, however, it is seen as something ordinary and unexalted that provides an entry, not into the dreamy world of pure spirit, but into the concrete reality of human beings. If in the earlier essay Unamuno seems to atomize or conceal individual defects in the dazzle of spiritual mist (the passage begins with a description of a fog that fuses all the distinct elements of the visible world), he here advises his readers not to hide their meanness and their vanity. "It is best to . . . let oneself be what one is, according to God's will, baring one's soul and following one's impulses."

Yet in this essay too there are moments when Unamuno comes close to the familiar self-defeating pattern of an over-eager defense. Carried away by his affirmation of the value of instinctive action, he says that only in combat can we learn compassion. From there it is a short step to the glorification of warfare as "the great purifier of rancor". At the conclusion of his argument in favor of work and action he gives us a rapturous description of faith in the self that recalls the inflationary rhetoric of "Plenitud" and "¡Adentro!"; once again we are told that pride is simply the confident sense of fullness which all men should aim at; acts are "spiritual offspring", and one must engender, gestate, and give birth, or else die. At the essay's end, we see that Unamuno again loses sight of the common, ordinary world of men because of an all-consuming need for self-assertion.

III

Ontological Greed: The Tragic Sense of Life

Feeling yourself a slave within
you sang of domination and it was a lament. . . .
("To Nietzsche", XIII, 611).

In *Del sentimiento trágico de la vida* (1913, XVI), the tension between Unamuno's incompatible aspirations becomes part of an ontological construction.
He begins by saying that all philosophical systems originate in the emotional
life of their authors, an observation that leads him not to philosophical rela-
tivism but to the claim that his own problem is, or should be, the most urgent
concern of all men (138). The longing for immortality is an obsession which
Unamuno attributes not only to other persons but to all reality. A central
feature of his philosophy is the confusion or fusion of the psychological and
the ontological – the notion of individual consciousness tends to merge with
that of being itself.[1] From Unamuno's own desperate compulsion to assure the
continuity, unity, and substantiality of the self emerges a vision of the whole
universe as a gigantic effort of autogenesis.

Because this philosophy of anguish springs from the most personal intuition,
from his "feeling about life itself" that has "subconscious or perhaps unconscious
roots" (129), the book's structure reflects that pattern of double oscillations we
have been observing. An argument is sometimes broken off unfinished as if the
author did not choose to reach certain unavoidable conclusions; significant links
that would clarify a given topic are not presented; as in the essays, positions
and perspectives repeat, alter, or reverse themselves so that the reader must
impose his own order. There are a few coherent sections, such as the one that
traces the history of the Christian idea of immortality (Chapter IV) and the
ones that painstakingly demolish the supposed rational bases of faith and the
traditional proofs of God's existence (Chapters V and VII), but many of the
book's most crucial events are imbedded in a web of passionate and obfuscating
language. The exposition circles around an unstable center and eludes its own
contradictions even as it formulates new paradoxes.

One of the first topics taken up is the derivation of human consciousness from

---

[1] Although François Meyer has stressed this fusion, he argues that the postulation of
universal conflict is not a "sentiment" or a "projection of temperament" but a "necessary
ontological structure", an odd disclaimer, especially in view of Unamuno's insistence
that the inner biography of a man is what explains most about his philosophy (128);
"our theories are usually the means by which we seek to explain and justify our acts to
others and to ourselves" (385).

the need for perpetual existence (Chapters I and II). Consciousness thus defined, says Unamuno, is a disease. But this infirmity is man's finest achievement
and greatest good because it puts him in touch with "higher" reality. Whereas
the instinct for survival has developed his intellectual faculties (knowledge –
conocimiento) and given him control over the visible world, the "instinct for
perpetuation" has developed spiritual faculties (*sentimiento*) and made possible
access to an ideal or invisible world that is created in fantasy. The purpose of
this distinction, which is not new here (see, for example "Sobre la filosofía
española", 1904) is to show that although immortality may be denied by reason
(a faculty he usually, but not always, associated with survival), it is affirmed by
desire and that we can ignore neither the negation nor the affirmation. In the
present treatment of the subject, however, the consequences of the two "instincts" become inextricably snarled for much the same reasons that isolation
and merging were brought together in the single idea of solitude. The principal
ambiguity has to do with the relation between knowledge and reason. Unamuno
places knowledge at the service of the "individualistic" instinct for survival, and
connects reason to man's "sociability" which is, in turn, derived from the instinct
of perpetuation (language, a social product, is the "father of reason" [155]).
Knowledge and reason would seem then to be at odds. Yet a few pages later
they are used interchangeably and synonymously in the assertion that knowledge and life (presumably immortal life) are incompatible because life is anti-
rational and the rational is the negation of life (161). As in those essays where
Unamuno articulated the casual sequence (1) desire for immortality and/or
fame, (2) enmity towards others, (3) sense of isolation, (4) longing for communion, he attempts here a description of the hunger for self-perpetuation in terms
of solidarity with others, hoping thereby to situate the cure in the very source
of his suffering. The competitive struggle for perpetuation is thus transformed
into the bond of love that unites men and creates society.

The dynamics of self-aggrandizement and self-annihilation become more
dramatic in Chapter III (titled "The Hunger for Immortality") which shows
that both the need and pursuit of fame are limited manifestations of an enormous covetousness (François Meyer speaks of "avidez ontológica") that is awakened by the terror of non-being.

> The visible universe is too narrow for me . . . it is like a cramped cell . . . I
> suffocate for lack of air. . . . More, more, and always more. I want to be
> myself, and without ceasing to be myself to be others as well, to merge with
> the totality of things visible and invisible, to extend myself to the limitlessness
> of space and prolong myself in the infinity of time. Not being all and for-
> ever is the same as not being . . . and to be the whole of myself is to be
> everyone else. All or nothing! (166)

And then, "what is not eternal is not real". The statement in "¡Adentro!" that
awareness of our "radical nothingness" is what makes us aspire to be everything,
has now stretched out its fullest meaning. The concern for immortality is rooted
in this primary ontological greed.

Yet the desire to encompass the whole world threatens the prized uniqueness
and separation of the ego, for if he were everyone and everything, he would

not be Miguel de Unamuno. Being all is as destructive to the self as being nothing; he might just as well have said "all is nothing". In a later passage, he contrasts reason and imagination for the way they take us to the limits of existence; reason is an analytical and dissolving force – it annihilates, whereas imagination makes whole and integrates; reason by itself kills and imagination gives us life. But imagination "by itself, in giving us life without limit, leads us to lose our identity in the All and also kills us as individuals, it kills us with an excess of life" (305-6).

Much of *Del sentimiento trágico* is devoted to working out various strategies for protecting the individual ego from this dual threat of extinction. Unamuno insists on his distinctness even as he "extends himself to the limitlessness of space". Eager to preserve the boundaries of the self, he repeatedly says that what he wants is to be both all the others and himself as well. At times, however, he is tempted by the idea of dissolution, as when, in a passage about the absorption of others, he momentarily envisions the peace of perfect union. "I love my neighbor because he lives in me and is a part of my consciousness, because he is like me, because he is mine . . . Oh, if only one could prolong the sweet moment and sleep and make oneself eternal in it ! . . . in this lake of quietude . . . insatiable desire sleeps . . . both hopes and fears have died !" (174). But the temptation immediately gives way to energetic repulsion. Forgetting that he was the one who was doing the swallowing, he sees the danger outside himself. "No, I do not want to drown in the vast All, in an infinite and eternal Matter or Energy, or in God." He wants not union but an impossible combination of identification and differentiation. "I do not want to be possessed by God, but to possess Him, to become myself God without ceasing to be I myself who tells you this" (174).[2]

The theme of ontological hunger leads to the theme of the hunger for fame which, we know, is derived from the first and is, in the last analysis, equally self-defeating. "Earth becomes hell with the appearance of the struggle for perpetuation" (183). All the same, Unamuno is no more willing to be relieved of the second compulsion than he is of the first – his description of modern man's obsession with fame shades equivocally into a justification of it. "Once hunger is satisfied . . . vanity, the need to impose oneself and live on in others, arises." But this survival is a matter of appearances only because fame is an insubstantial image in the minds of others. "We need others to think us superior to them in order that we may think so ourselves and thus support our belief in our own persistence or at least in the persistence of our fame" (180). To achieve this illusory guarantee, men strive to obliterate the remembrance of those who are already famous because "they rob us of our place". Yet Unamuno takes pains to deny any accusation of egoism that one might make by maintaining that the lust for renown is only a reaction to the terror of extinction. Vanity is at bottom

---

[2] According to F. Meyer's description, "what the existent would like is . . . impossible, the limited without limits and the finite infinite . . . 'to be the others without ceasing to be himself'. The contradiction is in the heart of being" (26); he says that the paradoxical formula, "serlo todo sin dejar de serse" ("to be everything without ceasing to be oneself") is dialectical (27), but all of Unamuno's writings make clear that this antagonism never moves beyond itself.

nothing but "eagerness for survival" (180); Herostratism is "longing for immortality" (183); and envy, which springs from the competitive struggle for fame is "spiritual hunger", a condition more painful than physical hunger but also precious evidence of moral superiority; only the strong yearn for immortality and "only the weak resign themselves to death" (this in a passage attacking Nietzsche's idea of the eternal return). Thus envy, greed, and vanity become positive spiritual values.

In protesting that "my health and strength urge me to perpetuate myself" (178) Unamuno transforms the gnawing inner emptiness and the dread of annihilation into proof of spiritual substance. As in "Plenitud" he attempts in this book to base the continuity of the self on pure desire. But first he must discredit the rationalist or scholastic argument that derives the substantiality of the soul from the feeling that one has an identity that persists throughout the transformations of the body. He speaks scornfully of the "spiritualist" theory of a transcendent "I" standing behind immediate experience as its source and unity. Reason should tell us that in reality there is nothing more than the living body with the states of consciousness it sustains. It is the body that thinks, desires, and feels. Unamuno does not want to accept "sophistical" arguments to establish the rationality of the belief in an immortal soul because for "scientific psychology", which he calls the only rational one, the unity of consciousness is simply a phenomenal unity; it is not a substance. The notion of substance is a "nonphenomenal category"; it is a noumenon and, strictly speaking, is "inconceivable" (213). The supposed rational bases of faith thus dissolve with the proper application of reason.

But if Unamuno wants to deny the validity of rationalist and "spiritualist" arguments for a transcendental unity of consciousness, it is in order to affirm that unity on the basis of feeling alone. The noumenon is unkowable but not, in his view, inaccessible. He is hardly ready to accept the evidence of "scientific psychology" although he has just used it to demolish faulty reasoning. Unamuno thinks that science destroys the concept of personality by reducing it to a complex in continuous flux, and he is eager to salvage that concept. What was denied in Chapter V becomes, in Chapters VII and IX, the heart of Unamuno's theory of consciousness – the unity and substantiality of consciousness is discovered and validated in suffering.

Chapter VII ("Love, Suffering, Compassion, and Personality") begins with a distinction between love and sensuality. Carefully separating the two, Unamuno identifies true love with pain. Pleasure and love are incompatible. The sexual act must always be at the service of perpetuation; to take pleasure as a goal is sheer covetousness[3] (far from making any connection between the body and pleasure he says, in another passage, that "perhaps we were given a body so that we would be able to feel pain"). But he also sees in the sexual act a momentary loss of self, a "splitting, a partial death" endured for the sake of "the sensation of resurrection, of being reborn in another" (261). Sex acquires

___

[3]In "Sobre la lujuria" ("On Lust", 1907, IV, 468-74), Unamuno contrasts passion and sensuality, saying that the development of the latter always leads to the stunting of spiritual life; the value of marriage is that by "eliminating disturbing desires" it leaves one "free for higher and nobler enterprises".

value for Unamuno either as a means of reproducing oneself (and for him this happens in the literal sense that makes the child the reincarnation of the parent) or as an occasion for experiencing the pain of self-estrangement.[4] Pleasure is repudiated unless it can be recognized as self destruction; when the delight of self-forgetfulness reveals itself as the torment of internal splitting, it is redeemed and justified.

But suffering that is totally spiritual is even better. Since sensual love unites bodies but separates souls, spiritual love appears, "with a sigh of liberation", when physical love has died. The first experience of such disembodied love, and its prototype, is, he says, the mother's compassionate tenderness for her child. This is what we strive to regain, to be once more an object of compassion and pity. One way of accomplishing this is to play oneself both the roles of parent and child. Unamuno describes the results of this internal duplication. "As you go deeper into yourself . . . you will discover more and more your own emptiness . . . you are not what you would like to be, you are, after all, only a nonentity. And on touching your own nothingness, on not feeling your permanent ground, on not reaching your infinity or your eternity, you will feel whole-hearted compassion for yourself, you will burn with a painful love of yourself, a love that extinguishes what is called self-love" (265-66). Clearly, the price of recreating within onself the compassionate mother is the reduction of the loved self to a "nonentity". But all other people are seen as equally insignificant – indeed, it is the revelation of a common insubstantiality that makes us love our fellow men who are "wretched shadows that pass from nothingness to nothingness, sparks of consciousness that shine for a moment in the infinite and eternal darkness" (266). We are able to love others by finding in them our own self-reflexive, self-destructive love. Compassionate love of oneself and of others thus dissolves everyone in a phantasmal mist that corrodes the very substance of the universe, uncovering the "tedium of existence, the bottomless pit of vanity of vanities". Through the vision of total illusoriness Unamuno reaches "universal compassion, universal love" (266).

At this point, he shifts suddenly from the theme of ideal love to the drive for conquest and dominion; the reader is able to supply the missing link because he recognizes both the need for compassion and the need for domination as consequences of the sense of inner insufficiency. "If it is painful one day to cease being, perhaps it would be even more painful to go on being always oneself and no more than oneself, without being able to be everything else, without being able to be all" (266). In the formula "all or nothing" the second term really refers to a person's concrete existence; Unamuno sees the fact of human limitation – individuality and mortality – as non-being. In comparison to his infinite aspiration, his actual self is not simply diminished but obliterated. "Seek yourself, then. But on finding oneself, does one not discover one's own nothingness?" (365).[5]

[4] "The pleasure of reproducing oneself – in flesh or in spirit, in children or in works – is an ecstacy, a rapture, an estrangement, a deathly pleasure. Death and resurrection" (Prologue to El hermano Juan, 1935, XII, p. 875).

[5] F. Meyer (op. cit. 27, 36) and Julián Marías (Miguel de Unamuno, Madrid: Espasa-Calpe, 1943, p. 199) would not agree; both see the insignificance of the self as a comparative term; they do not follow Unamuno to the extreme of his thought.

The pain of this humiliating realization is, however, our most valuable experience because only through it can we attain "reflexive consciousness" – for Unamuno the only true consciousness – the "consciousness of one's own limitation". Suffering is the hallmark of consciousness; it is the "substance of life and the essence of personality because only through suffering is one a person." Pain is also, we saw, proof of true love. "In this world one must choose between love, which is pain, and pleasure . . . As soon as love is satisfied it is no longer love. Happy, satisfied people do not love." Thanks to suffering we know that God exists and that we exist. "We do not know we have a soul until it pains us" (a statement that Augusto Pérez repeats in *Niebla*). Pain is not merely the means of achieving consciousness – it is the only conscious experience. Feelings and acts that take us out of ourselves make us unconscious. "When we enjoy ourselves we forget that we exist, we become other . . . we become estranged from ourselves. And we take hold of ourselves, return to ourselves, only by suffering" (268). When Unamuno says that man's supreme pleasure is acquiring and heightening consciousness, he is talking about pain. In the earlier essays, there was no mention of the role of suffering in the search for the inner self; here it is the requisite for self-possession : anguish makes consciousness turn back upon itself. The person who is not anguished, "thinks but does not think that he thinks and it is as if his thoughts were not his own. Nor does he belong to himself. For only through anguish and the passion for immortality does a human spirit take possession of itself" (339). God too, the eternal and infinite consciousness of the universe, is the painful knowledge of His own boundaries. Suffering is the "limit that the visible universe imposes on God"; it is the wall that consciousness runs up against as it strives to extend itself in space and time (338).

Since consciousness is defined as the wish to be everything and the simultaneous awareness of limitation, consciousness is pain. Yet thanks to suffering, "one grows ceaselessly in consciousness and longing" (380). In such a scheme, the loser always wins. Consciousness is the will to be eternally defeated and frustrated. As François Meyer says, the "sadism of being" demands not only the acceptance of an eternally renewed agony but also the desire to cultivate and nourish it. Since eternal happiness would obliterate consciousness, Unamuno asks, why not an eternity of suffering?

According to this account, consciousness is not only invariably painful but also necessarily reflexive – the picture is one of masochistic solipsism. Consciousness is not directed outwards; it is not a grasp of the world or of otherness but only the tortured awareness of its own struggle to maintain itself. In an early essay ("El individualismo español", 1902-3) he had written that a consciousness of consciousness with no object but itself is impossible; he now makes the desire of that impossibility the sole criterion of consciousness. Because total reflexiveness also characterizes his idea of love, of personality, and of God, each term can stand in place of any other; they are all interchangeable references to a single reality, which is, moreover, the only reality – consciousness. Obviously if consciousness is defined as the eternally frustrated effort to seize itself, there can be nothing beyond it. "What is not consciousness and eternal consciousness, conscious of its eternity and eternally conscious, is nothing but appearance. The only thing that is truly real is that which feels, suffers, pities, loves, and desires, the only thing that is truly real is consciousness; the only substantial thing is consciousness" (282).

The psychological conflict is the ontological one. But just as obviously, the definition of consciousness as perpetual frustration cancels out its supposed "substance". The contradiction of "Plentitud" is fully elaborated as the central paradox of *Del sentimiento trágico de la vida*. The ultimate substance turns out to be the painful awareness of insubstantiality. "Consciousness, the craving for more, always more, the hunger for eternity and thirst for infinity, the appetite for God – these are never satisfied" (339). Reality is the desperate longing to come into being. "Universal suffering is the anguish of every being to become all the others without ever succeeding . . . The essence of a being . . . is not only the effort to persist forever . . . but also its effort to universalize itself; every created being tends not only to preserve itself but to perpetuate itself as well and, moreover, to invade all other beings, to be the others without ceasing to be itself, to expand its boundaries towards infinity, but without breaking them" (334). François Meyer almost understates the case when he defines Unamuno's notion of being as "insubstantiality and radical insecurity" (83). Unamuno's universe is a ghostly lusting after its own elusive being.

The early chapters of *Del sentimiento trágico* show the consequences of this central paradox for individual psychology. Threatened at once by "all" and "nothing", conscious man strives to swallow the whole universe and yet maintain the contours of his private self. The chapters on religion (VIII, IX, and X) show the conceptual maneuvers entailed in constructing a religious ideal that avoids the mortal hazards of finiteness and infinity. For one thing the creative process must be open-ended and incomplete : man creates God by endeavoring to believe in Him (321) and God, in turn, creates himself in and through man (297). But the very idea of God becomes problematical, for how can there be an infinite consciousness if consciousness by definition presupposes limitation? Unamuno poses the question but does not answer it; the whole of Chapter X is a series of such unanswered and unanswerable questions. "Could not apocatastasis, the return of everything to God, be an ideal which we unceasingly approach but never reach? . . . Would not absolute and perfect happiness be an eternal hope that would die if it were realized?" (369). He wonders what would become of each individual consciousness in the final union of souls. "What about me, what about this poor fragile self, this self that is the slave of time and space? .. . Would I resign myself to sacrifice this poor self of mine?" (380). Earlier he had energetically rejected any union that would destroy his uniqueness. "Wanting to unite with God is not wanting to be lost and submerged in Him . . . the complete dissolution of the self in the dreamless sleep of Nirvana; it is wanting to possess Him rather than to be possessed by Him" (369).[6] He yearns for reunion with Christ – and yet, "my soul, mine at least, yearns for something else, not absorption, not quietude, peace, and

---

[6] In the Diary he wrote that "dying in Christ is fusing with all others" (p. 11). In *En torno al casticismo,* he said that the Spanish mystic seeks not to drown in God but to possess Him (III, p. 260); "stripped of all desire" he remains "as a potentiality for everything" (p. 259) – in other words, totally free.

obliteration, but an eternal approach . . . endless longing, eternal hope . . . and with it an eternal lack of something and an eternal suffering" (381). In other words, an eternal Purgatory. The eternity of peace, gratification, and perfect delight means loss of self. Unamuno wants time – only in time can he preserve the painful sense of separation and incompleteness that tells him that he exists. "Do not destroy time!" (381).

Although Unamuno acknowledges the essential contradiction of the desire to "be everything without ceasing to be oneself" both in relation to individual psychology (in the chapters on fame) and to religious theory, he manages to elude the contradiction on which much of his system rests – the vacillating distinction between reality and appearances. When he says that "the only true reality is consciousness" (that which "feels, suffers, pities, loves, and desires") and that "what is not consciousness . . . is nothing but appearance", he sets reality against appearance. But when he describes reality as the anguished longing to appropriate substantiality, he collapses or inverts that distinction. Consciousness, which at one moment is "the only substance", becomes in the next, insubstantial appearance ("you will love all your fellows and brothers in the world of appearance, those wretched shadows that pass from nothingness to nothingness"; 266). But then he reaffirms the opposition when he says that the torment of being a mere shadow proves that one is substance. And so on. Unamuno never indicated that he was aware of these dizzying reversals just as he never formulated the paradoxical conclusion that plentitude is absence. But he cannot for long endure the conflict of his two antagonistic wishes; inevitably he reaches the point where, in an ever repeated gesture, he abandons the anguish of acknowledged contradiction in favor of a rapidly alternating presentation. A, then B. Or else A is called B.[7]

Unamuno's critics have also tried to work their way around this contradiction. François Meyer, for example, says that since consciousness is by definition limited and finite and since "what is not eternal is not real", Unamuno must reach the conclusion that all being is devoid of substance and condemned to illusoriness; he connects this to the theme of life as a dream which is central in Unamuno's works. Meyer repeats Unamuno's assertion that the substance of an individual's being is its very insubstantiality – life is pure longing to be – and he concludes that man can only make or imagine himself – the human mode of being is, in Unamuno's phrase, a fictitious entity". This "terrible revelation" frees us, says Meyer, from the mirage of being as substance and reveals "being-as-fiction" ("el ser-ficción"). Man must continually dream himself into being. Thus, paradoxically, the imagination is "the most substantial faculty" and living is like writing a novel.

In summarizing Unamuno's own arguments, Meyer has for the moment to ignore the fact that Unamuno was also very eager to make a distinction between reality and appearance. So too, most of Unamuno's commentators who fit the

[7] Carlos Blanco Aguinaga has written that in most of his works Unamuno avoided "true contradiction" by insisting only on the inner world and that up to *Cómo se hace una novela*, his thought characteristically moved by "the alternating affirmation of opposites" ("Interioridad y exterioridad en Unamuno", *Nueva Revista de Filologia Hispánica*, VII (1953), pp. 605, 701).

"life is a dream" motif into an existentialist creed (each person is the fictional character he spends his life creating) seem to forget Unamuno's frequently expressed horror at the "hypnotic sense of life and the world". Either you oppose reality and dream or you confound them and say that reality is a dream. Unamuno does both alternately, which makes us suspect that the fusion indicates an attempt to protect the self from the real hazards of the outside world and other people – and from his own internal contradiction. The transformation of everything into dream or fiction (and this will be more evident later) is simply an escape from an intolerably conflictive reality.

Chapter XI attempts to show how the lack of dogma can provide a basis for practical morality. From his ontology of instability and insecurity, Unamuno derives a precept for action – a variation of the advice of Senacour's Obermann – "If nothingness is our fate, let us live so that it will be an unjust sentence" (387). And to do that, we must impress others so that they will remember us. We should strive to be "irreplaceable, stamping our seal and mark upon others, acting on our fellowmen in order to dominate them; giving ourselves to them in order to make ourselves in some measure eternal" (392). Just as Montarco's terror of non-being whetted his appetite for invasion, Unamuno's discovery of his own "nothingness" gives rise to a dream of conquest and domination. "True religious morality is at bottom aggressive, invasive" (404), even "inquisitorial" (405). Each person tries to make himself divine, to immortalize himself by dominating others –"All Gods and all masters!" (407). "We must stamp others with our seal, perpetuate ourselves in them and in their children, dominating them . . . The most fertile ethic is that of mutual imposition" (401).[8] "He who does not lose his life will not win it. Give yourself to others, but in order to do that, dominate them first . . . one cannot dominate without being dominated. Each one nourishes himself with the flesh of those he devours" (402). As in "Soledad", he preaches mutual assault in the name of true communion.

Unamuno does not explain how this domination is manifested or just what it involves except that "in order to dominate one's neighbor one must know and love him". He then describes love as a fusion with the other. "To love my neighbor is to want him to be like me, to be another me, that is, to want to be him; it is wanting to erase the dividing line between him and me." Love is the effort "to be and live in him and through him and make him mine – which is the same as making me his" (402). The problem though (which Unamuno does not present) is how could one dominate a person who has become indistinguishable from oneself? If he is I, there is no one else. There would be no one to offer resistance or give recognition – or be dominated. The love which Unamuno describes would entail the destruction of the loved person as a separate being; it would simply be a kind of solipsism. As he wrote in another context, "in

---

[8] In a speech made in 1909 Unamuno described the hero, the "creative factor" in human history, in almost identical terms, "the energetic and brilliant individual who attempts to impose himself and stamp others with his seal". But there was no mention there of "mutual imposition" and the notion is plainly elitist (Cf. Elías Díaz, El pensamiento político de Unamuno, Madrid: Tecnos, 1965, pp. 68-9). Unamuno, none the less, frequently argued that his "ethic of imposition" was "the most altruistic and universal" one. "I do not preach a pure I, like Fichte's . . . but an impure I which is myself and all the others as well" (X, p. 333).

order to use something or dominate it, it must remain distinct from me" (272). He could have argued, on the model of the aspiration to be everything without ceasing to be oneself, that love is the movement towards fusion with the other but that the goal is never reached. Instead he chooses to make fusion (apocatastasis) "a norm of action". Unamuno's idea of love, whether conceived as compassion for oneself or as this obliteration of personal boundaries, is invariably a negation of otherness.[9]

But fusion with the loved one destroys the individuality of the lover as well – in the previous chapter he had worried about what would happen to "this poor fragile self" if the ideal of apocatastasis were fulfilled. Here he seeks to forestall the danger of dissolution by describing merging as an intensification of the pain of consciousness. And consciousness, we know, is always "feeling oneself distinct from other beings" (268). Thus "invasive charity" bids me offer to others my suffering as nourishment and consolation for theirs; I must arouse their anxiety with my own. Unamuno wants to awaken others to "anguish and spiritual torment" (405). Thus he counters his longing to lose himself in others with the torture of being forever mutilated and estranged. In one famous passage the two aims meet in an ecstasy of pain. "Do not take opium but put salt and vinegar in the wounds of the soul because when you sleep and do not feel pain, you are not. And one must be. Do not close your eyes to the terrifying Sphinx, but look at her eye to eye and let her seize you and crush you with her hundred thousand poisonous teeth and swallow you. And when she has swallowed you, you will know such sweet, such delicious suffering" (406). Look the Sphinx in the eye but do not answer her question. Unamuno does not want to acknowledge what man is. Rather than accept limitation and mortality, he will let himself be torn by those poisonous teeth; to evade death, he courts destruction. The choice was already prefigured in the Diary when he spoke of suicide and wondered if his obsession with nothingness was not simply "pure egotism".

The passage also underscores another feature of the duality of isolation and merging in Unamuno's work – his tendency to phrase it in the vocabulary of oral aggression. It is, after all, the "hunger and thirst for immortality" that drives each man to "nourish himself with the flesh of the one he devours". In Cómo se hace una novela he says that the characteristic of true individuality consists in "nourishing oneself with other individualities and in giving oneself to them as nourishment" (X, 849). Dominating means devouring and the pleasure of that act alternates with the ineffable delight of being devoured. The old poet had said, "I do not want to devour others. Let them devour me. How beautiful it is to be a victim! To give oneself as spiritual food . . . to be consumed . . . to dissolve in the souls of others" (II, 749). In Niebla, one of the characters hits on the idea of a doubled and fully self-contained pleasure – one should devour oneself. The postulation of ontological hunger seems to lead to a vast cannibalistic feast. One of Unamuno's characters says, "cannibalism is the perfect thing, believe me, anthropophagy. Man can only live off other men. . . . we must eat souls, which are . . . most painful to digest. Feed on them and give

[9] Pedro Laín Entralgo says that for Unamuno the other is an imaginary projection or duplication of oneself (Teoría y realidad del Otro, I, Madrid: Revista de Occidente, 1961, pp. 145-56).

your own as food" (IX, 831). But one problem, which Unamuno does not acknowledge, is that if I devour the other, there will be nothing left to eat; this is the dilemma that confronts many of Unamuno's fictional characters. Another problem is that swallowing everything is the same as being swallowed up, and even if he describes being swallowed by the Sphinx as "delicious suffering", the dynamics of *Del sentimiento trágico de la vida* make abundantly clear that either process would cancel out the sense of individuality Unamuno so desperately needs. The endless oscillations between contrary goals mean perpetual craving; the self that hungers after God and immortality is a bottomless pit, that can never be filled up.[10] He can only hope to create through language the illusion of inner substance; he will suggest spiritual bulk by sheer force of words, by an incantatory piling up of those terms which are so dear to him – substance, flesh, blood, entrails, pith, marrow, food. [11]

[10] We are reminded of the description of the schizoid self given by R. D. Laing in *The Divided Self* (London: Penguin, 1966), p. 145: "one might call it an oral self in so far as it is empty and longs to be filled up. But its orality is such that it can never be satiated by any amount of drinking, feeding, eating, chewing, swallowing". Carlos París (*Unamuno, estructura de su mundo intelectual*, Barcelona: Ed. Península, 1968) says that Meyer's reference to "avidez ontológica" recalls the "avidez oral" of psychoanalytical terminology (p. 352).

[11] For a different reading of those words, see José Ferrater Mora's chapter on "The Idea of Reality" in his *Unamuno, a Philosophy of Tragedy* (Berkeley: University of California, 1962).

IV

Fragmentation and Doubling

Self-duplication, Unamuno once noted, first occurred when early man caught sight of himself in the still water of a pond and came "to know himself outside of himself, to think of his self and then to believe in his soul" (X, 111). In *Del sentimiento trágico*, he argued that the concept of an immortal self arose in order to preserve the continuity of personality. Against the felt discontinuities of life, one can postulate a model of permanence; the self is not a constantly shifting locus of perception, feeling, and thought, but an immutable entity as complete and whole as the person seen in the looking-glass.[1] From this idealized image of perfect stability, it is but a short step to the metaphoric identification of mirror-image and eternity. Thus Unamuno describes his wife as a "virgin mother" who is his "holy mirror of divine unconsciousness, of eternity" (X, 885). Such a mirror does not so much reflect the self as enclose it; he imagines himself in a virginal womb that is forever closed to the world of time and mortality. In *San Manuel Bueno, mártir*, he also used the mirror as a symbol of enclosure and immortality; the mountain and village of Valverde de Lucerna are reflected in the waters of the lake and duplicated in the mythical village said to be submerged in its depths. Real world and magical one form a perfect and containing circle that is a figuration of eternity.[2]

Much more characteristic of Unamuno's use of the mirror analogy, however, is the description of a nightmarish estrangement. Since the looking glass gives back the image of a body which itself misrepresents the inner life, it shows something doubly unreal. If Unamuno likes to believe he is not his body, surely he cannot be its illusory reflection. Yet the denial makes him confront himself as "another", a "stranger". He sometimes regards his own personal history as a kind of looking-glass phantom; whenever he thinks of himself impersonally, he feels "the terrible sensation of the doubling of personality, of becoming a spectator of my own person" (X, 241-2). That vision and the mirror image are often used interchangeably to represent doubling; the crux of the matter is seeing oneself as another. In *Niebla* Víctor Goti says that when he stands before

---

[1] Jacques Lacan describes a "mirror phase" in the development of the conception of the self. The gestalt of the total body, seen first in the others and then in the mirror, "symbolizes the mental performance of the I, at the same time that it prefigures its alienating destination" (*Écrits*, [Paris, Sevil, 1966] I, p. 91).

[2] The cluster of ideas that Unamuno weaves around this image is exceedingly complex. For if the lake is the model of eternity, it is also the possibility of annihilation – Don Manuel's temptation to commit suicide. And suicide can, in turn, represent the possibility of salvation. Angela says that Don Manuel taught them to "submerge ourselves in the soul of the mountain, in the soul of the lake, in the soul of our people – to lose ourselves in them in order to remain in them" (XVI, 624).

the mirror "I finally doubt my own existence and, seeing myself as if I were another, I imagine that I am a dream, a fictitious entity".[3]

The source of uneasiness in these experiences is the equation of self and other because for Unamuno the substantial existence of the other person is always in doubt. In "Soledad" he knows the other becomes a phantasmal projection of his own consciousness; the visible person then must be a lifeless apparition. "There are moments when I seem to be alone and the others seem to be nothing more than dreams, ghosts that move and speak."[4] In "Soledad" he speaks of empty shells that "by a strange magic, move, talk, and act". So when he looks in the mirror and sees himself as "another", the hallucinatory vision corrodes his own substance. If the cultivation of reflexive consciousness empties the world of bulk, substituting the subject's fantasy for the objective presence of others, being "another" means ceasing to exist. In the Diary he wrote "I remember looking at myself in a mirror until I imagined myself duplicated and saw my own image as that of someone else. How sad that is! It is like being submerged in unfathomable waters . . . going towards nothingness, towards eternal death" (84). If the others are phantoms, the self as other is also phantasmal. His body becomes inert matter; he once said that hearing himself on a phonograph record and seeing himself in a mirror produced the impression of "having an interview with my dead body" (IX, 989). Sometimes he turns others into fictitious beings, at other times he directs that disintegrating gaze at his own concrete self. He depopulates the world, or rather, he transforms it into a ghostly duplication of himself.

We remember that when Unamuno converts others into his imaginary vision of them, it is in order to include all relations within his own consciousness. That he was aware of the ultimately self-negating character of such an enter-prise is evident in a short story called "The travels of Turismundo" ("Las peregrinaciones de Turismundo", 1921, IV, 293-97); the first part is "La ciu-dad de Espeja" (which could be translated "The City of Mirrors"). A traveler, about to die of hunger, thirst, and exhaustion ("hambre, sed y sueño" – the last word is suggestive and ambiguous because it also means dreaming), comes upon a strange city surrounded by an invisible but impenetrable wall. Finding its single gateway, he enters and sees spacious streets through which a few mys-terious empty vehicles move; there is no one in the houses, gardens, or public buildings. Although he is tormented by loneliness, he has the uncanny feeling of being touched by thousands of invisible glances, and he thinks he hears the echo of silent laughter. The streets seem crowded with people he cannot see, hear, or touch; calling out to them, he discovers to his horror that he cannot hear his own voice. "It seemed as if the atmosphere so saturated with men, made up of them . . . drowned his voice and with it himself." He wishes for "true solitude – which puts one face to face with God and far from oneself" and which can be achieved only "in the midst of the noise and bustle of people". In the cemetery he meets an odd dwarf who says he is his servant and who explains that the only person in the entire city is Turismundo himself – the

[3] Madrid: Austral, 1958, p. 114.
[4] Letter to Ilundain; quoted by Hernán Benítez, *El drama religioso de Unamuno*, p. 278.

invisible multitude is his own image duplicated thousands of times. The dwarf himself is only an echo, a sounding board for the lonely wanderer.

The story indicates (though Unamuno draws no moral) that the person who searches for the self (and wears himself out "dreaming") ends in isolation and immurement, in an empty fortress, haunted by fantasies that threaten to stifle and destroy. The permanent identity which the subject seeks continually eludes him, mocking his efforts with endless fragmentations and reduplications.

Recognizing the dangers of the solipsistic quest, Unamuno countered his own "derealizing" tendencies with the argument that "No one knows himself if he does not know the other. Only through others can one know oneself. Because folding in upon oneself . . . and living in self-examination is the way to forget oneself, to empty out and become separated from one's own being" (IX, 1017). And he described a "social self" which is the "reflection that the world gives back to us through myriads of mirrors – our fellow men". Frequently, however, even the effort to know oneself through the other becomes a reflexive exercise in which the other's consciousness is reduced to the status of reflecting agent. The aim shifts from mutual recognition and affirmation to what he called in the Diary "seeing oneself from the outside", in the mirror of other people's eyes.

The eye as a "living mirror" was one of Unamuno's favorite metaphors. Precisely because the real mirror is so frightening, he seeks confirmation in another consciousness : "our best mirror is each one of our fellow men . . . One does not know oneself except in others . . . Even though the image of ourselves in the pupils of others' eyes is very tiny, it is the seed of self-knowledge" (XI, 800). The smallness of the reflection facilitates, as one perceptive reader has observed, "the illusion that the viewer is again a child",[5] an impression reinforced by Unamuno's preference for the word *niña*, as opposed to *pupila*, for the pupil of the eye. In the eye of the other, one can be both parent and child. A character in *Amor y pedagogía*, thinking about the girl he loves, says "Today I have seen myself . . . in those immaculate eyes; today I was in them, tiny, feet-up, huddled in the round pupils (*niñas*) of her virginal eyes" (II, 369). In *Dos madres* when Raquel kisses her reflection in her lover's eyes, she is trying to get at herself. And when Augusto Pérez, the bumbling solipsist of *Niebla*, tells the laundry girl that he wants to see himself ("so tiny") in her eyes in order to "know" himself, it is clear that his goal is the rapt possession of his own beloved image.

To find oneself in the eyes of others is, according to Unamuno's interpretation of Cervantes's novel, the quixotic enterprise. It is also the real aim of Don Juan's amorous adventures. In the prologue to his last play, *El hermano Juan* (1929), Unamuno explains that Don Juan devotes his whole life to the creation of an image in the eyes of others. He says that even if we accept the view that Don Juan's eroticism is fundamentally onanistic, we would have to describe it as a self-love that requires mediation. "At most Don Juan enjoys himself . . . outside of himself, but in the imagination of others . . . And this is where vanity enters. And with it, history, legend" (XII, 869). In other words, history itself is the

---

[5] Lucille Braun, " 'Ver que me ves' : Eyes and Looks in Unamuno's Works", *MLN* 90 (1975), 212-30.

process of mediated self-regard and its motive force is vanity – the desire "to be seen, admired, and leave a name".

If man makes himself exist only through the gaze of others, without their looks he vanishes. He needs their collusion to support his existence – alone he faces an empty mirror. "The person who does not exist in others and for others, the person who does not portray himself, does not exist . . . he lacks personality. And when he looks into the mirror, he does not see himself" (V, 1191). In *Cómo se hace una novela*, Unamuno says that since "the legend, the novel" about Miguel de Unamuno which he and his public have made together is the source of his identity, he cannot look for any length of time into a mirror : "I feel myself emptying out, losing my history, my legend, I feel as if I were returning to unconsciousness, to the past, to nothingness" (X, 864-5).

Yet even the collusive support of others fails to maintain the precarious sense of reality in a world that has become a hall of mirrors. In a newspaper article on insomnia ("En horas de insomnio", 1911) Unamuno says that though it is sad to pass one's life contemplating oneself like a fakir, it is perhaps even more sad to look at others and see only oneself. If the others are mirrors of the self and the self also a mirror, then there is nothing but mirrors reflecting other mirrors with nothing in between – no content, no concrete existence, no body. "And this is the worst solitude." He includes a sonnet which tells how he can find nothing human outside of himself in which to affirm himself; he is hollow, an empty prison in which he fears he will sink and lose himself; he is a hermit shuttling between mirrors, bereft of human company. He feels that he is dying and that one day, "mirror of mirrors", he will find himself estranged from himself, completely lifeless.[6]

Thus the pursuit of the self in the reflecting gaze of others leads ultimately to total isolation and the dizzying sense of his own "nothingness". This, we know, intensifies Unamuno's enormous ontological hunger. The mirror experience heightens the desire to absorb all otherness or, alternately, to be absorbed by what is other. The sequence can be seen in the early play *La esfinge* (1898); the protagonist sees himself in the glass as an alien figure ("A shadow. No. I am alive, alive !") and then says that he wants to "swallow up the universal spirit" – or else be swallowed up : "My God, submerge me, drown me, that I may feel my life dissolve in your breast" (XII, 250). He turns from an hallucinatory vision to the affirmation of self-destruction. Faced with an empty looking-glass, he longs for annihilation.

*   *   *

A writer's past history is found in his works. They reveal him. But in so doing, Unamuno often felt, they also betray him. He sometimes saw his words – and indeed all words – as a kind of alienation. He also held, however, the contrary view – that the talent of the true speaker or writer is his ability to create a thoroughly original language that at once communicates ideas and transmits the personal matrix in which they take form. He talks about a friend who was "so full of spirit, so full of himself", that, even when he used the most ordinary

[6] Manuel García Blanco, "Don Miguel de Unamuno y sus poesías", *Acta salmanticensia*, Tomo VIII (Salamanca, 1954), pp. 180 and 399.

language, he seemed to be inventing it (III, 799). According to this view, language is an actualization of the speaker, and a man's thought and expression are rooted in his whole life experience ("our philosophy springs from our feeling about life itself"). Thinking is necessarily tentative and perspectival. "An idea has value only in a man's spirit." They are not "fixed, stable, immutable entities" but adaptable and plastic forms that are modified by each person who receives them (III, 639). Through the process of transformation ideas enrich a collective spirit in which the speaker can ultimately recover his thought (III, 598). A conceptual system should not be a logically articulated mechanism but a living organism with the internal discordancies that life creates and resolves (III, 1060).

Unamuno wants his own written style to preserve the flexibility of thought that comes into being in advance of speech ("the form always develops after the essence"; III, 583). The speaker must invent his own language as he uses it. "Others try to fit their concepts into the words of the common store; I want to make my language fit my thought" (III, 752). Thus, he insists, the best philosophical expression is metaphorical.[7] Even obscurity is valuable because clarity is the characteristic of dogmatism. Spanish, a "language of conquistadors and dogmatic theologians", lacks nuances for the expression of the inner life. In En torno al casticismo he related the clear Castilian air to the incapacity of Spanish artists to create subtle shadings or a lifelike "nimbus". The good writer, the one who is able to pour out "the sap of feelings and desires" is "misty" (neblinoso, III, 798). Clarity, which kills "the indeterminate, the shadowy, the vague, the formless, kills life" (III, 593).[8]

Yet Unamuno believes that language constantly moves towards ossification and that the growth of an idea is menaced by the tendency to rigid formulation. "The word, which first protects the idea, often ends by smothering it" (III, 586). Unamuno is in favor of neologisms and of all kinds of linguistic barbarisms because they help break up the hardened patterns of thoughtlessness. But his view of the inexorable drift of language towards dogma and lifeless simplification results finally in his seeing it as the antagonist of thought. Thinking itself is then situated in the realm of wordless feeling. Because he fuses thought and sentiment into an ineffable inner experience, speech becomes empty verbiage – hollow shell or crust. All the familiar oppositions between inner and outer, living and dead, full and empty (Unamuno speaks of two kinds of style, that of the guts and that of the covering) are brought in to portray language as the betrayer of the heart's desires. Unamuno sees the expressive act as one that unavoidably involves us in duplicity, and the written work as a haunting and tormenting double.

This is the view elaborated in an early essay, "Intelectualidad y espiritualidad" (1904, III, 701-17). It opens with a description of a writer who is alone in

[7] Unamuno's own style is not especially metaphorical and his favorite images – the substance and guts ones – far from embodying the flux of reality, point to an implicit ideal of stability and solidity, an ideal that, ironically, forever threatens to come true; the yearning for internal substance is matched by the fear of sclerosis. The only movements described by his metaphoric language are the throbbings and pulsations of entrails.

[8] See Juan Marichal, "La voluntad de estilo de Unamuno y su interpretación de España" in his La voluntad de estilo (Barcelona: Seix Barral, 1957), 217-32.

his study, enjoying a sense of communion with the familiar objects around him, "that square glass ink-well, those thick pen-holders, that folder, that heavy leather chair . . . all of them were like an extension of his spirit and at the same time they were arms that the world extended to embrace him. They were he and yet they were other". The feeling of solidarity is suddenly destroyed when he reads a manifesto he had once written, a paper in which he had "emptied his spirit" but which now seems strangely foreign. He cannot believe the words are his or that he had thought in that way, yet the manuscript is undeniably his and it has, moreover, won him considerable renown. It must be, he thinks, that language itself deformed his ideas. "As soon as thought is incarnated in words . . . it is someone else's, or rather, it is no one's because it is every one's. The flesh with which language is dressed out is communal and external; it darkens thought, imprisons it and even turns it around."

He is reminded of another disturbing experience, when he saw himself in the mirror as "an insubstantial shadow, an ethereal phantom". The work is a double. As Unamuno said in another essay, in literary activity he often feels as if he were "pursued by a mirror" (VI, 615). At other times the self shatters into multiple fragments and he thinks he might have within him "a legion of sleeping souls". Whether the written word dissolves the self or duplicates it, the unity of the ego is destroyed. Cut off from himself, he wonders (like the acquaintance in "Soledad") if others see him as he does; often ("only too often") as he goes down the street calm and composed, it occurs to him that he is really leaping about ridiculously or "committing shameless acts". He decides that the cause of these dissociating episodes lies in the nature of action and speech – they are both means of self-estrangement. "My thoughts are never exclusively mine . . . nor is the language I must use to make myself understood mine . . . Am I myself mine? And the tormenting obsession returns." Unamuno comments that life is a continual struggle between "our spirit that wants to take possession of the world . . . and the world that wants to get hold of our spirit and make it the world's". In this "tragic battle" each enemy tries to engulf the other, yet each one also needs the other in order to maintain his self. "Everything I say, write and do, I must say, write and do through the world"; the world depersonalizes consciousness so that "I appear to be another person that I am not".[9]

According to this account, thought and speech are separate systems. Language is not a way of acquiring significations that would otherwise remain vague and blurred but an external medium that the speaker must use in order to translate his pre-existing thoughts. The translation is always deficient. Merleau-Ponty said that in language "I experience that presence of others in myself or of myself in others that is the stumbling block of the theory of intersubjectivity".[10] Unamuno's conception of language is a good example of the problem because he sees the presence of others as an intrusion. "What a wretched task

---

[9] In "Civilización y cultura", written in 1896, he also discusses the relations between self and world but instead of a tragic battle and violent acts of appropriation and destruction, he describes a process whereby the two interpenetrate and mutually create each other; he refers to the "communion of our consciousness and the world" (III, 473). Blanco Aguinaga (*Juventud del 98*) sees the influence of Marxist thought in this early essay.

[10] *Signs*, trans. Richard C. McCleary (Evanston: Northwestern University Press, 1964), p. 97.

it is to write! What a sad compulsion it is to speak! Between two people who speak, there is an intervening medium of language that belongs to neither one of the speakers, and that intruder envelops them, and at the same time that it brings them together, it also separates them. If only it were possible to create language in the very process of speaking what is thought!" In another place he wrote that words belong to the world, not the speaker, and that in order to express a sentiment or a thought that springs from the deepest part of the self we have to use the language of the world, "but the inner fountain, the intimate and invisible substance, comes from the roots. . . . Language is society's – but the sap is mine" (III, 1032).[11]

Faced with the opposition of language and sentiment that would seem to make impossible any genuine exchange of words, Unamuno yearns for "the substantial communion of souls". Perhaps, he thinks, what cannot be formulated in language can be imparted in some other way; people might understand each other simply through their "spiritual presence" (he once wrote to a friend: "Why can't souls communicate with each other directly, without signs?"[12]). In a lyrical interlude he tells how once, in the country, he listened to a peasant boy singing and felt a kind of mystical transport as if hearing "the voices of the other world that throbs within our world". The writer, he says, can convey some inkling of such ineffable experiences through metaphorical language. And that is why imagination is the highest faculty and why poets are better than men of science or action (for Unamuno art and science often represented the opposition between inner truth and deceptive surfaces – "through love we reach things with our whole being and not just with our minds . . . and from this art is born". III, 181). Poetic speech takes one beyond the ordinary world into the "entrails" of things. The essay has turned full round and the self-estrangement produced by reading his own work is overcome in the ideal of the union of souls in art. The price of the writer's renown was alienation, but the way back to integration is through the imaginative work; once again the isolation of fame calls up the nostalgia for fusion.

One consequence of Unamuno's expressionist view of poetry is that the literary work acquires value not as an autonomous event in the world but as the vessel of the poet's soul. The poet does not simply make a work, he pours out his soul – literature is always confessional. "The most precious thing is to give oneself . . . by baring one's soul" (IX, 837). The poet is the man "whose flesh escapes from under the shell, whose soul oozes out" (III, 890). Even in a philosophical essay, what counts is self-revelation : "the thesis is what is least important in such a work. It is an occasion for spilling out one's soul."[13] The writer writes in order to expose himself not only to others but to himself as well : "through style we discover ourselves" (XI, 840). "I write in order to affirm

---

[11] The protagonist of *Niebla* has an even more negative view of language. "As soon as man talks, he lies, and as soon as he talks to himself, that is, as soon as he thinks and is aware of his thinking, he lies to himself. There is no truth except physiological life. The word, a social product, was made for lying . . . Each one of us only plays his role. We are all personae, masks, comedians" (p. 96).

[12] Hernán Benítez, op. cit., p. 279.

[13] *Epistolario a Clarín*, p. 103.

my personality before myself. It is a way of getting to know myself."[14] The writer also writes in order to get into the hearts of others, and the reader reads in order to discover the author's inmost feelings – the goal of literary activity is alternately self-possession and spiritual communion. "Only by making themselves one, can novelist and reader save themselves from radical solitude" (X, 922). Since fusion in Unamuno's thought so frequently presents itself as a mutual devouring, it is natural that he should call the novel a living organism with "entrails throbbing with life, warm with blood" waiting to be consumed by the reader ("when a book is a living thing, one must eat it", X, 841).

But if the writer offers himself as food to others, he destroys himself. The process through which he hopes to save himself in others is a form of suicide. In objectifying and making perceptible his inner life, the artist loses it. "My thoughts . . . broken off from their emotional root . . . and fixed in unalterable forms, are cadavers of thoughts" (XVI, 217). As he said in "El secreto de la vida", one must not expose the inner sap and source to the light of day. "As soon as a thought is fixed in writing, expressed, crystalized, it is already dead . . . Literature is nothing but death" (X, 830), though a death from which others may draw life and through which the writer himself hopes to win an after-life; in a peculiar but telling metaphor, he once referred to his poems as his children from whose breasts he wants to "drink perpetuity" (XIII, 207). But over and over he returned to the notion of the work as a means of self-estrangement. It keeps slipping away from him – its language is not his and it shows an uncanny and alarming independence; existing in the world, and accessible to others, it cannot really be the same as the psychic force that produced it. For this reason, perhaps, Unamuno sometimes tried to prevent his works from coming to any conclusion. "My God, may this essay never end; may my life never end!" (III, 805). The unwillingness to let go of the story might account both for his disdain for plots and for the self-reflective structure of those fictions (*Niebla*, "Don Sandalio") in which he tries to suggest a continual, never-ending circular relation between reader and writer. Certainly this is the motive behind the central thematic image of *Cómo se hace una novela* – the novel that can never end.

Unamuno also believes that the artist may also literally lose himself in his creation by misrepresenting his feelings. Even with total good faith, Unamuno says, the writer is bound to transform and deform feeling; he cannot hope to be sincere because art itself is the beginning of insincerity. "The sincere thing would be to stretch out in the country, look at the landscape and not describe it."[15] The question of sincerity would pose no problem if it were not that Una-

---

[14] Cited by Birute Ciplijauskaite, *El poeta y la poesía* (Madrid: Insula, 1966) p. 171.

[15] Letter to Corominas (*Correspondence*), quoted by Catalán, "Tres Unamunos . . .", p. 69, note 95. We can find many contrary statements about sincerity and about its relation to art. "The duty of sincerity commands us to conceal our insides because if we revealed them others would see them as something different, and thus we would be lying . . . the more sincere a soul is, the more jealously it guards and shrouds the mysteries of its life" ("El secreto de la vida", 1906, III, 1031). "Man's highest virtue should be sincerity" ("Mi religión", 1910, IV, 387). "I believe that all, absolutely all of the evils that we think cause our wretchedness, egoism, the desire for prepotency, the eagerness for glory, the disdain for others, would disappear if we were honest" ("¿Qué es verdad?", 1906, III, 1004). In the same essay he says "there is nothing farther from the

47

muno's theory of art makes the work the uncovering of the artist's inner self. Thus any elaboration might be judged a falsification. He wanted to "spill out his soul" but he could not help seeing that the moment he put pen to paper he was guilty of artifice. Furthermore, he was very much worried about the possibility of bad faith; the artist might fabricate a personality to suit the needs of his literature and cultivate emotions for their aesthetic yield. The protagonist of *La esfinge* complains that he can find no solace in any experience whatsoever because he immediately turns it into literature. "I do nothing but play a role. I spend my life watching myself, turned into theater" (XII, 227-8). The expressive act, ironically, means the corruption of life. Unamuno frequently accused himself of playing to the gallery – and just as frequently, especially in later works, he justified that by saying that the theatrical role *is* one's life. At all times the notions of literary production and histrionic representation are entangled and even used interchangeably. The artist is an actor, a man who plays himself and fashions his own mask. "I was a circus number . . . I am becoming a comedian, a buffoon, a professional with words. And even my sincerity . . . is turning into a rhetorical topic" (IV, 312). The doubling is a process he cannot control and, as we shall see, the final solution is to attempt a new identification with the double itself. Literature is histrionics, but histrionics are the truth of life – this paradox, which Unamuno called "the terrifying problem of personality", is the unifying theme of the late works.

---

lie than art" (999-1000). And, in "Soledad", "the poet is the man who has no secrets from God in his heart . . . when he sings his sorrows, fears, hopes and memories, he strips and cleanses them of all deceit" (III, 887). The reversals are, of course, grounded on the dichotomy of inner self/external image.

V

The World Stage: Acting, Fiction, Fantasy

The dynamics of the two oscillating patterns – inner self/outer self; isolation/ merging – grow increasingly convoluted as we move from the early essays, through *Del sentimiento trágico de la vida*, to the works published in the nineteen twenties. The strategies required to give some semblance of consistency become ingeniously devious. By making an analogy between life and play-acting Unamuno endeavors to present the tormenting experience of doubling and internal cleavage as the affirmation of authenticity and wholeness. In his earliest works (for example the play *La esfinge*, 1898) he was fascinated by the figure of the actor, but from the twenties on, the theme becomes central. Stage acting is seen as the prototype of all human action and the imaginary deed is made to seem real. But the conceptual acrobatics needed to maintain this position turn our attention to familiar emotional and intellectual splits.

One of the most revealing comments is the short fictional piece called "Robleda el actor" (1920, IX, 289-92) about an actor who disconcerted his public because, while always successfully filling his role on stage, he somehow suggested absence; on one level he seemed to be outside of the scene. In spite of his obvious absorption in the character portrayed, people felt that there was something else, that behind the role, Robleda was acting out another and deeper tragedy. Playwrights disliked him because he subtly transformed the characters they created, and other actors were reluctant to play parts he had made so much his own. Little was known of his private life. To the narrator, however, he once confessed his secret – he was horrified by the thought of exhibiting himself. "I hate to be the focus of the gaze of so many people and I would like to make myself invisible, sink into the earth. My greatest concern when I go on stage is that the public might see me, Octavio Robleda . . . that is why I am so careful to characterize myself so that my own personality is erased." That is the tragedy he is playing underneath the public one, and Robleda emphasizes the fact that this hidden drama too is play-acting. In childhood he always wanted to be invisible and now he tries to hide from prying eyes in the characters he represents. Behind his obsession is the fantasy of self-possession. "I want myself for myself and only for myself." Only concealed can he be free. "Why do they seek me out? . . . I know how to play Hamlet or Segismundo or Don Juan or Don Alvaro, who are exhibitionists, spectacular men . . . but myself? I do not know how to present myself. I am always trembling for fear of being ridiculous. Nothing is more repulsive than the buffoon." Hating the theatricality of life and dreading the mockery of others, he takes refuge in the theater of art. Those who accuse him of pride do not realize that it is nothing but a shield for his timidity : he is driven to the stage out of "the horror that others might see me, notice me, that they might look at my gaze and thus steal the secret of my solitude". The desperate need to possess the self is accompanied by the fear of its being stolen. In *Del sentimiento trágico,* Unamuno expressed this fear as his "supreme anguish"; "With Michelet I cry : 'Mon moi, ils m'arrachent mon moi !' " (XVI, 173).

Robleda uses the role as a mask but others may use personality as a mask. Unamuno often described it as such. In order to have a personality, he said, one must play oneself so that others can see the character. "The man who does not exist in others and for others, the man who does not act [el que carece de representación] is not, . . . he lacks personality. And when he looks into the mirror he does not see himself" (V, 1191). Robleda's strategy, according to Unamuno, is not only very common but also absolutely essential to life; existence can be assured only by being visible to others. "Being is the same as being perceived. And we should add, making others perceive the one we are" (XVI, 274). Although Unamuno's works from the beginning show his preoccupation with fame as the guarantee of perceptibility, he increasingly conceived of all human actions purely in terms of appearance. The person who gesticulates before an audience "represents" himself, that is, he conjures up an image of himself. Unamuno used the word "representation" to refer both to the role played and to the mental picture others have of the performance. And everyone – except those who have no "personality" (in the earlier terminology, those who lack "substance") – plays a role. Unamuno was fond of reminding his readers of the etymology and the evolution of the word *persona,* which first signified a resonating mouthpiece, then the mask used by the actors, then the character represented in a drama, then the role each person plays in society, and finally, "the stage of our own consciousness" (III, 319). Acting in society and in history are both forms of play-acting. "Human society is nothing but a theatrical company . . . and the social self is nothing but a hypocrite." Historical man is "the one who plays his role on his stage, in his little world, the one who plays the actor, the hypocrite" (V, 1192).

What is behind the mask? "It is true there is the self one thinks one is and the self one wants to be; but there is also the self that others think one is and the one they want to be. And this is the role, which is imposed. . . . And the duty of each person is to play as best as possible the one that falls to him". The actor and his mask is Unamuno's last formulation of the dichotomy between inner and outer selves and, like the others, it permits no solution or reconciliation, though, like the others, it lends itself to certain rhetorical manipulations which suggest the fusion of opposites – even if, as we have seen repeatedly, that fusion is ever in danger of separating out into its original and incompatible components. Thus in one essay he claims that human nature is completely a matter of appearances and that one is only what the others can see because "in private the only thing that acts is one's individuality or animality". Then, in the same discussion, he reverses himself and says that "the fundamental, essential, intimate and therefore lasting self of each person is what one wants to be and not what one is" (V, 1196). On the one hand he is only his public image, on the other, he is not really what he "is". In Sartre's terms, he shifts between thinking of himself as pure "facticity" and thinking of himself as pure transcendence, the two movements of bad faith. Both are abstractions that deny the mixed conditions of existence.

But calling oneself an actor is a more complicated trick than equating the self with external appearances. The actor is conscious of creating an appearance and therefore conscious also of being something else. Unamuno says one must learn his role so well he forgets he is acting. Yet as soon as a man defines himself as an actor, he remembers his duplicity. One cannot be a hypocrite without misrepresenting one's "private" self. The "animal" cannot be an actor.

Professor Sánchez Barbudo has said that Unamuno's theatrical analogy is a confession of duplicity.[1] He does not, however, talk about the dissimulation involved in the confession itself. On the other side of the polemic are the critics who see the theme of theatrical "representation" as evidence of Unamuno's supposedly existentialist philosophy : man makes himself by acting on the stage of the world. Thus when Unamuno says we are all hypocrites, one critic, beguiled by Unamuno's own rhetoric, says that he is simply calling attention to the public nature of human actions; his purpose is "to advance the idea that hypocrisy can be an authentic mode of existence".[2] But Unamuno's position is at once more honest and more profoundly self-deceiving. On some occasions he seems to take others to task for deluding themselves : he once wrote to a recent convert to Catholicism, "you seem to be an actor, a sincere and perhaps ingenuous actor, but an actor. You are playing (*representando*) or rather, playing yourself (*representándose*) as a convert on the stage of your own conscience" (XVI, 935). But more frequently he defends hypocrisy as true self-expression. "Hypocrite means nothing more than actor. And the actor portrays a feeling in order to animate and maintain it . . . every man who is truly conscious is playing himself on the stage of his own consciousness"(IX, 1046). At other times the breach between inner and outer selves just barely opens and the hypocrite is seen as the man who is trying to get at the reality of his own pretences; "There are hypocrites who profoundly feel the role that they are acting and would like to be what they pretend they are" (V, 1191).

If, as Hegel said, in a true act the "individual is for others what he really is", in a theatrical act he retains a meaning and intention that are not manifest. Since the actor assumes his roles, he lays claim to the freedom to do so. "He" is not what he seems to be; he is only pretending. Because he can observe his own performance, he can put himself in the position of others, of the audience. And then he can go back to the stage. Back and forth. He imagines himself away from his acts and then imagines himself back at them. He thus retains a total, if illusory, control. In the Diary Unamuno said that if we identify fully with the role, ignoring the reactions of the public and playing only for personal satisfaction, we are guilty of "masturbatory pride" (178). The arrogance consists of an admission that is immediately withdrawn, so that the actor simultaneously divulges the "truth" about himself and suggests that he is really different – much better – than his observable being.

In the actor's capacity "to play at what he is doing, 'he' sets himself at one remove from his actions as they are observable and definable to another. In this

[1] See *Estudios sobre Unamuno y Machado.*
[2] Paul Ilie, op. cit., p. 71.

way he eludes the others, and in a sense eludes himself simultaneously".[3] In emphasizing the theatrical nature of his acts, he seems to take responsibility for deception while really exonerating himself. If I claim to be a hypocrite, but devoted to my role, then I can enjoy the advantages of detaching myself from my acts while denying that I am doing any such thing. The actor thus gains surprising freedom not only from others but from the consequences of his own deeds and words. As Sartre says, "that is the aim, to put oneself out of reach. 'I am an actor; nothing can touch the actor.' "[4]

Beyond the reach of others lies the desert of solitude. The price paid for total evasiveness is loss of feeling and the company of one's fellows. The actor wins complete control of a dead landscape. Or, as Unamuno said in one of his sonnets, by playing his role he is made into his own theater, where he is "the king of the desert" and everything around him is stiff and lifeless. He eludes the touch of the world but he himself is turned to stone.

*   *   *

In 1924 Unamuno was exiled to the Canary Islands for his persistent political attacks against the dictatorship of Primo de Rivera and the event won him national and international acclaim. After a few months in Fuerteventura, he fled to France where he established himself in Paris in voluntary and, it turned out, lonely exile. He had acted in accordance with the legendary independence and rebelliousness of Miguel de Unamuno and the consequence was isolation from his family, his countrymen, and his public. He must have been at that time intensely aware of the price paid for renown. The work which reflects the crisis of this period – the dilemma of the inner self vs. the historical role – is *Cómo se hace una novela* (*How a Novel is Made*, X, 827-923).

The main part of the book was written in 1925. In 1927 Unamuno included a Prologue, a Commentary on Jean Cassou's Introduction to the 1926 French translation, many passages intercalated in the body of the text, and a Continuation. The central portion, which has been described as a "personal novel" and a "novelistic autobiography",[5] combines an essay (on literature, time and eternity, history, role-playing, hypocrisy) and a hypothetical novel whose structure and plot are discussed with the reader. The novel might be called a metaphorical version of the central topic of the essay – the relation between a man and his history or legend. The Prologue, Commentary, and Continuation consist of additional observations on the novel and on some themes of the essay.

Unamuno begins the book proper by announcing to the reader that he is writing in order to snatch himself away from death and become "eternal or immortal"; he will spill out his life so that he can continue living (857). Balzac's *Peau de chagrin* had given the idea for a novel that would also be an autobiography, though he points out that every true fiction or poem is autobiographical because all the characters in fiction or, for that matter, in historical works as well, are parts of their authors; even the historian puts himself into the figures

---

[3] R. D. Laing, *Self and Other* (London: Tavistock, 1961), pp. 27-8.

[4] *St. Genet*, trans. Bernard Frechtman (New York: Mentor, 1964), p. 388.

[5] Ricardo Gullón, *Autobiografías de Unamuno*; Armando Zubizarreta, *Unamuno en su nivola* (Madrid: Taurus, 1960).

he describes. Thus the characters of Unamuno's personal historical drama, the Spanish politicians and leaders with whom he clashed, owe their existence to him. "Are they not as much creatures of mine . . . as Augusto Pérez, Pachico Zabalbide, Alejandro Gómez, and all the other creatures of my novels?" (862). Since literature is inevitably autobiographical, its invented personages are as real as living men and women (as he often said, Don Quixote is as real as Cervantes). In fact Unamuno talks as if literary reality were the only one. "Everything is a book, a reading." There is the Book of History, the Book of Nature, and the Book of the Universe. "In the beginning was the Book. Or History. Because History begins with the Book and not with the Word. And before History, before the Book, there was no consciousness, no mirror, there was nothing. Pre-history is unconsciousness, it is nothingness."

If History is created in books and does not exist outside of them, the written word determines what happens. The historian, Unamuno says, can provoke events because he makes men believe in the objective reality of what he has described. "Winning a battle is making others, friends and enemies, believe it is won. There is a legend of reality that is the substance, the inner reality of reality itself" (863). The essence of a people is the philosophy of history that it constructs in order to make sense of what happens. The same is true of the individual. Through reflection and interpretation events become facts (*hechos*, literally, "things made") and we progress from what "happens and passes" to what is "made and remains". This distinction recalls the one between history and "intrahistory", and in both cases the referent of the first term fades before the "substantial" and permanent reality of the second. "What is made, is made in consciousness." Reality is the recreation of incidents and people in writing.

These ideas could be part of a perspectival view that would set varying interpretations (the historian's "fictions") against each other – or they could indicate an illusionistic thought that absorbs the concrete world into the written word. The latter is Unamuno's. He plays upon the double meaning of the Spanish word *historia* – both history and story – because he is trying to turn external "facts" into things he alone has made. Thus, when he goes from the topic of history in general to that of the individual's history (or legend) he uses the idea of the unconsciousness of pre-history to support his claim that the external self is the real one (as he said in *Del sentimiento*, "what is not consciousness is nothing but appearance"). The disquisition on history and historiography serves as a preparation for the more crucial examination of the personal history of Miguel de Unamuno.

A writer's historical self is constituted by his books and their public reception. Since the violently polemical Unamuno has become legendary, his "novel" has been created jointly by himself and others. His fame is his whole being and without it he is nothing ("And that is why I cannot look at myself in the mirror . . . I lose my history, my legend, my novel and return to unconsciousness of the past, to nothingness", 865). Yet we know that he cannot really accept that public self; he hates to think that without his history he would cease to be. He wants to believe that there is another, invisible self behind the legend, an "unknown and unknowable self" which the novel threatens to destroy. "This history devours me and when it ends I will end with it" (864). The historical role, through which he dreams of "making himself eternal", is precisely what promises to annihilate the hidden self. His anguish is that he must kill himself in order to live. "This Unamuno gives me life and death, it creates me and destroys me, sustains me and smothers me. It is my agony. Am I what I think I am or what others think I am?" (865).

The novel he proposes to write is at once an analogy to the problem of the two selves and an attempted solution. Unamuno, the author, will make himself eternal through the story of a man who is living alone in exile in France, a character whose situation would represent his own. This man, Jugo de la Raza (Jugo was Unamuno's maternal surname), is lonesome and terribly bored because he is confined to that "poor self underneath history . . . the sad man who has not made himself a novel". He likes to read novels in order to live vicariously in others, "to be another, to make himself eternal in another", but also "to discover himself, to live in himself, to be himself. Or rather to escape the self that is unknown and unknowable even to himself" (866). Both Jugo and Unamuno look for identity and eternity in the novel, and in both cases that means self-estrangement and the radical separation of inner and outer, unknown self and "novel".

One day Jugo buys a book at one of the bookstalls on the Seine. It is a novel, a "romantic autobiographical confession". As he reads, he loses himself so completely in the book that ordinary reality disappears; when he lifts his eyes to look at the river, it seems to have stopped flowing – it is a "motionless mirror". "Horrified he looks away and returns to the book, the novel, in order to find himself, to live in it" (867). This reminds us of Unamuno's own frightening experiences before empty mirrors. In the book he reads this warning: "When the reader reaches the end of this painful history, he will die with me." Jugo discovers that he cannot live without this book; he dares not read it and yet he has to. Meanwhile, Unamuno, the author who is, he says, every bit as "novelistic" as his character, recalls that he first thought of writing this story at a time when he found it difficult to write or do much of anything else because he was immobilized by the fear of "being devoured by my acts" (868). Jugo's fear and Unamuno's fear hold them back from their novels – the one cannot read, the other cannot write. Therefore *Cómo se hace una novela* never becomes more than an account of *how* one makes a novel, never the real thing.

Unamuno carefully builds all the conceptual bridges between Jugo's situation and his own so that the reader cannot help but constantly refer the supposed fiction to Unamuno's internal debate; we read about Jugo only to learn what Unamuno is saying about himself. Thus, when Jugo feels that "time is devouring him, that the future of the novelistic fiction was swallowing him", when he forgets his unhistorical self so completely that he can say it has "died" (872), we know that Unamuno is representing his own fear of being consumed by his acts. Jugo transmits the modulations of his author's thought. If at the beginning Unamuno was able to say that one's legend is made in collaboration with others, in the story about Jugo he shows us a novel (the one Jugo bought) that seems to be bringing itself into existence before the reader's eyes. "The other was a dream that dreamed itself in him, a creature of his infinite solitude." Jugo is possessed by that dream and as he struggles with his demon book, Unamuno worries about sacrificing his "inner self, the divine one, the one I am in God, the one that should be, to the other one, the historical one". "Am I not making my legend, the one that buries me? . . . But if I do not make my legend, I will die completely. And if I make it too."

In an effort to cheat death and acquire an objective and enduring self, both Jugo and Unamuno seek to identify with an external legend. But this means splitting themselves in two, and all subsequent efforts to bring the two parts together only result in further cleavage. *Cómo se hace una novela* shows the failure of every attempt to solve the dilemma of inner self vs. legendary self. The most characteristic ploy is to deny the split itself. "Hypocrite? No, my role is my truth and I must live my truth, which is my life. . . . Am I acting out a comedy, even for those closest to me? But no! My life and my truth are my role" (884). There is no difference between inner and outer, between truth and role. Everything is outer, everything is theater – or novel. The historical situation of Spain becomes the scene of a fiction which is Unamuno's drama; historical personages are incorporated into his fantasy, so that Primo de Rivera and Martínez Anido are "creatures of my spirit", fictitious beings who live only within him. "Do they exist, in any way, outside of myself?" (882).[6] The opposition between history and story is dissolved as Unamuno's real, objective antagonists are made part of his subjective truth. He is the only actor, his is the only novel.[7]

Yet that novel threatens to kill him. History means the destruction of the individual. Time is tragedy and the novel is – alas! – only a novel. The feelings of a person who lives only for literature are spurious. He quotes Mazzini : "I know those sorrows of artists that artists describe; they are the shadows of pain and not its substance." But, adds Unamuno, only shadows exist. The semblance conceals nothing. When we see that all emotions are only the "shadow of tedium" we reach "the depth of the novelistic tragedy, of the tragic novel of history . . . pain is shadow and not substance" (886). Unamuno had advanced the argument that all life is a novel and that all acts are hypocritical (or theatrical) in order to ward off the terror of insubstantiality, but the argument seems to turn against him – the novel, the theater – all life – becomes shadow, not substance. "Life is a dream." We cannot even be sure about the emotional import of this vision. He concludes, "the noumenon invented by Kant is the most phenomenal thing imaginable . . . the depth [or essence] of a thing is surface" (895-6). Is this desperation or liberation?

As for Jugo, he cannot finish his novel; if he finishes it he will die and if he does not finish it he will die because the book has become his life. "One death or the other; in history [the story] or outside of it" (887). He tries to trick death by reading almost to the end. And Unamuno for his part chooses not to tell how the novel about Jugo would end. "Why finish the novel about Jugo? This novel,

---

[6] A. Zubizarreta calls this denial of independent existence love (op. cit., p. 862). Of course in Unamuno's novels love is generally portrayed as appropriation.

[7] Unamuno refers disdainfully to a woman writer (writing is a man's business) who tried to get publicity by linking her name with his; "preoccupied with her name" she tried to make "her novel", not his. The only novels that he tolerates are written ones, the one about Don Quixote, the one about Rafael Valentín, etc., because they become part of his spirit and "nourish him" (cf. "when a book is a living thing, one must eat it").

and all those that are made and not merely told, does not, strictly speaking, end. What is finished, what is perfect, is death, and life cannot die" (896). The pendulum might swing forever – the novel is death, the novel is life – Unamuno must leave it all inconclusive, hoping against hope that "life cannot die".[8]

Surrounding the unfinished novel about Jugo de la Raza and the essay that comments on it, are sections added in 1927 – the Prologue, Commentary, and Continuation. They enlarge on the central image of life as fiction, and the Continuation introduces a new topic – the nostalgia for what Unamuno calls "the eternal childhood of my spirit . . . my blessed childhood, my historical eternity" (905). Yet he also refers to the ideological contrary of this notion – the identity and eternity achieved in works : "our work is our spirit and my work is myself which I am making day by day . . . every man is the child of his deeds" (909). Against the eternity of childhood stands the personal history or legend which the writer fabricates in his books. "Did not Amiel live his life by telling it? Is not his Diary his life?" (917).[9] In the Commentary he also deals with solitude which is "the essence of our existence" and which we cannot overcome no matter how much we crowd together. This radical solitude, says Unamuno, breeds envy (842).

The various topics are not arranged in any particularly coherent way; Unamuno skips from subject to subject, presenting what seems to be a series of disconnected thoughts and opinions. But the themes are familiar ones and the reader might find in them a characteristic pattern as well. Thus the ideal of the inner self – the childhood one – seems to call up the ideal of the self made in and through the literary work. And the isolation and envy that come with the pursuit of his legend prepare the reader for a nostalgic description of fusion. Indeed, the whole self-absorbed tone of the 1925 original seems to call for some kind of countermove towards union with others. It is on this note that Unamuno ends the last section, saying that the writer writes in order "to make himself one with the reader. Only by making themselves one do novelist and reader save themselves from radical solitude. As soon as they make themselves one, they actualize themselves and thereby make themselves eternal" (922). Literature is, finally, not death but eternity. We now see the full implication of that statement at the beginning of the 1925 portion that "everything is a book, a reading". For Unamuno the ultimate salvation of the self is literary and communal, and words, written words, are the only reality.

And yet – Cómo se hace una novela is about literature as alienation. In the 1927 Prologue he says : "In my hotel room at no. 2 Rue Laperou I consumed myself and devoured myself in writing the narrative entitled Cómo se hace una novela" (827). Putting thoughts, dreams, and feelings into words "consumes them, kills them." Only History, the eternal present, lives. "Literature is nothing

---

[8] I do not agree with Carlos Blanco Aguinaga when he says that Unamuno's effort to resolve the contradiction eternity/time; interior/exterior, resulted in "the anguished presentation of the insoluble agonic contradiction that man is" (697-8). He believes that in this book Unamuno shows the inner and the outer as an "indestructible unity" (608-9). But Unamuno can no more close the breach than Jugo can close the pages of the novel. ("Interioridad y exterioridad . . .").

[9] In 1907 Unamuno had thought otherwise; he wrote that intimate diaries are the enemies of true intimacy (IV, 493-4).

but death" even if from that death others can take life (830). We realize that the dream of immortality was from the start also the nightmare of annihilation.

The main section of the book represents Unamuno's effort to exorcise the nightmare and affirm the dream. He tries to reunite himself with his "novel". He would like to show us that he is, after all, the author of the legend about Miguel de Unamuno. That is why he does not actually write the novel (the tense of Jugo's story is conditional throughout) because once they are written, novels are more or less autonomous entities; he will show us *how* they are made. By limiting himself to this hypothetical task, he can be sure that the reader, undistracted by a fictitious narrative, will focus only on the author and what he has to say about how novels are made and how life is lived. His formula for the book – "the creation of the creation, the novel about the novel, God of God, *Deus de Deo*" (865) – draws attention to himself as prime creator and sole master of his world. This formula, however, is also a means of evading literary commitment entirely. If literature is death, he can stay on the safe side by describing to the reader a possible work that never comes into existence. It looks like an elaborate attempt to protect himself from the judgment of his public, since one cannot evaluate what is only a supposition. As he said, he did not write, out of fear of being devoured by his acts. The hypothetical novel alludes to but does not define the secret self that "is" underneath the one that acts. And this elusive maneuver must be linked, in turn, to the message of the book itself; by insisting that he is his role and that this role is his truth, he assumes the devious innocence of the actor – he disclaims responsibility for his acts at the very moment of identifying himself with them.[10]

While protecting himself from the creative, and therefore compromising, act, Unamuno also protects Jugo from both life and death by keeping him in the realm of pure potentiality. Jugo is not the protagonist of a story (a fictitious history) because his dilemma is nothing but a reflection of Unamuno's own; it contains no element that cannot be re-phrased, through a simple set of equivalences, as Unamuno's personal problem. The "novel" about Jugo is a transparent artifice and we slide right through it. Jugo does not "live" as a character because Unamuno uses him for exclusively non-fictional aims. His "story" is not a fiction but an expository device in an essay on the hazards of fiction.

Unamuno, none the less, would have us believe otherwise. He talks about *Cómo se hace una novela* as if it were a kind of fiction. And the formula "novel about the novel" confounds fiction and essay. This confusion is the book's whole point – fiction is truth. Since comedy, play-acting, and legend are the words Unamuno uses to describe reality, he cannot be expected to distinguish between essays and novels or between the assertions of discursive prose and the non-assertions of literary fictions. Yet he advances the fusion as a truth. It is an assertion, not a theme developed fictively in a novel. He would undoubtedly be ready to play the circular game about the fictitiousness of such an assertion, but

---

[10] We might make a postscript to *Cómo se hace una novela* with this passage from an essay written in 1931; the legend is "not the wrapping or the outside, but the skeleton and the heart of reality". It is "the perennial historical reality, not the deceitful documentary reality" (X, 943). It is as if he said, "only the surface is real because only the surface is the depth and not the surface".

his claim for its acceptance is precisely what keeps the narrative about Jugo de la Raza from being a fiction.

Cómo se hace una novela might also be characterized as a kind of half-completed fantasy or day-dream. A person who says that everything is fictitious might be advancing an all-encompassing perspectivism that would reveal the illusory status of all ideas – fictions that are consciously recognized as fictions free the mind from the bewitchment of "truths". But a person who says and wishes to believe that the only truth is fiction, moves towards an all-encompassing fantasy in which thought creates its own reality and "winning a battle is making others believe it is won". The kinds of fictions – or for that matter, non-fictions – written in either case are quite distinct. The first (ironic, "perspectivistic") involves an obvious display of invention but an equally obvious skepticism about the relation between story and author. Instead of making his tale the vehicle of cherished beliefs, the writer delights in indicating the tentative and fantastic nature of all beliefs. Such narratives (for example, Borges's stories and essays) can be eloquent demonstrations of the creative and deceptive aspects of fictions, literary and non-literary alike. The writer would never defend fiction with the argument that it is the deepest, most "real" reality. On the other hand, the fiction writer who does use that argument might have trouble giving shape to fiction, providing it with a plot and a beginning and an end. The story might remain a strange hybrid of day-dream and essay.

Frank Kermode has distinguished between fictions and myths. "Fictions can degenerate into myths when they are not consciously held to be fictions. . . . Myths call for absolute, fictions for conditional assent." A fiction is "something we know does not exist but which helps us to make sense of and to move in the world."[11] In *Cómo se hace una novela*, we witness the effort to create a myth of history as fiction. And the Continuation suggests another myth – the magical fusion of reader and author that makes them both eternal. He once described himself as "a myth that I am making of myself day by day . . . and my task is to make a myth, to make myself a myth. The end of life is to make oneself a soul" (X, 512). Of course, Unamuno wants us to understand that such a personal myth is the truth of existence. In the Continuation he says, "I myself am my work" (909).

The end of life ("fin de la vida", both goal and ending) is the beginning of immortality. The self will live on as myth in the minds of others. Unamuno says Jugo's novel has no ending because "life has no end". But the beginning is as much a terminal point or boundary as the end. In scorning both the beginning and the end, Unamuno prevents his character from coming into being – to escape death, you avoid life – and exchanges the possibility of fiction for the equivocation of a never completed exercise in fantasy. In the Commentary he said that some readers might find the book like a set of Japanese boxes, one within the other and the last one empty. "But that is the way the world is – commentaries on commentaries and then more commentaries . . . Inside the flesh is the bone and inside the bone is the marrow, but the human novel has

---

[11] *The Sense of An Ending* (London, New York: Oxford University Press, 1966), pp. 39 and 37.

no marrow, it has no plot. Everything is . . . dream" (853).[12] It is worthwhile saying the obvious, that precisely because life has no plot, men seek "signs of order and form" in literary plots.[13] Besides, it is one thing to suggest the randomness of experience through a "plotless" or "open-form" novel, it is quite another to say that you *would* write such a novel.[14] An open-form work invites, through a rich ambiguity of structure and style, multiple interpretations, but Unamuno's assertion that truth is fiction allows no such proliferation of meanings.

The narrator of *Cómo se hace una novela* circles around the last empty box, never daring to abandon the realm of the virtual and the dreamed. The final fiction is the myth of personal immortality through literature ("spilling out my life in order to go on living", 857). To maintain that myth Unamuno is ready to engulf the reader's real world with his fantasy – Martínez Anido, Primo de Rivera, Spain under the dictatorship, the separate lives of his readers – all become part of the author's dream. As Sartre says of Genet, "he wants to take the real into the imaginary and drown it there".[15] The image of the world as fiction turns inside out – Unamuno is the one who is dreaming everything and everyone. In order to identify with his own novel, he makes everything "novelistic" and unreal. He aims at being the supreme and only fiction.

---

[12] In the epilogue to *Amor y pedagogía* Unamuno describes his procedure in creating the characters of that novel: "I have taken the hollows and covered them with words and acts." And this is the way real people are constituted too; all we can find beneath the words and deeds, beneath "the iron of our flesh", is "a hollow or more or less cylindrical hole".

[13] Kermode, p. 115.

[14] Inés Azar argues for the essentially modern and open form of this work in "La estructura novelesca de *Cómo se hace una novela*", *MLN*, 85 (1970), 184-206. On the open-form novel, see Umberto Eco, *Opera aperta* (Milan: Bompiani, 1962).

[15] *St. Genet*, p. 399.

VI

Dreaming

In his Diary Unamuno identified the "dream of life" with the vanity of worldly aspiration and achievement; he used it synonymously with "comedy" as a term of denigration. In the early essay "La vida es sueño" ("Life is a Dream", 1898) he retains the traditional sense of that Baroque topos, arguing that we must turn away from the temporal and devote ourselves to the eternal; in the context of this essay, which deals with Spain's social problems (the full title is "Reflections on the Regeneration of Spain"), that means turning away from any concern with change and reform.

The play *La esfinge* (*The Sphinx*, XII, 213-312) shows a similar disdain for historical and concrete reality, but the image of the dream is replaced by that of sleep – both are *sueño*. The protagonist is a man who is terrified of death and, though he knows that the terror springs from his obsessive and prideful cult of himself, from what he calls his "monstrous egoism", he has always sought to overcome it by making himself into a theatrical spectacle ("I spend my life watching myself, turned into theater") and living for his name in fame and glory.[1] Since such efforts only heighten his fears, he decides he must suppress ambition and attain peace through the dissolution of the self. Paradoxically his flight from death leads him to seek it out (he moves from the image of death as an "immense eternal emptiness" to that of dreamless sleep). Because he is nothing, he says, he wants to lose himself in the All, not, as Unamuno said in *Del sentimiento trágico*, in order to absorb all otherness, but in order to obliterate the painful sense of self, "to enjoy the peace of everything". Death is the reversal of individuation; it is a return to the womb (Unamuno often described death as *desnacer*, "to be unborn"). He speaks of melting into "the universal song of love of the Father", of being drowned, smothered and consumed in God's breast. Having lived like a rebellious angel (his name is Angel) "full of himself in satanic pride" he wants God to take him in his lap like a father so that he can "feel the warmth of his immense breast, the rhythm of his breathing, so that I can see myself in his gaze, in that clear pure sky and live in peace". God's eyes reflect nothing; like the mirror of eternity, they promise unconsciousness and loss of self. The yearning for absorption is also expressed in the wish to regain his infancy and become the child of his wife. Sleep and dream are the alluring symbols of reunion with the mother (or Father, because the imagery used in either case suggests the sheltering womb; the title points forward to that passage in *Del sentimiento trágico* about the "delicious suffering" of being chewed in the mouth

---

[1] His friend Ilundain wrote to Unamuno that the character was a "photograph of his author and creator" (Hernán Benítez, op. cit., p. 289), and many of the incidents Angel recounts are those of Unamuno's own life (see especially pp. 294-5).

of the Sphinx, though the sphinx is nowhere mentioned in the play). "Put my life to sleep, Eufemia, sing me a lullaby" to bring "endless sleep" – and peace. Unamuno's first title for this work was to be "Glory or Peace" and he had also considered "The Peace of Death".[2] Between glory and a peace which is death, between the actor's insubstantial farce and the dream of annihilation, there is no middle term – there is no life. The God to whom Angel prays is the negation of life.

The opposing images of the theater of life and the sleep of eternity reappear in the play *Soledad* (1921, XII, 588-621) which presents a playwright whose demonic ambition is to be all things and persons to himself. "Author, actor, public ... Father, Son and Holy Ghost. And one true God. I myself!" He talks constantly about creating himself and by that he clearly refers to his image in the minds of others – he needs the mirage of the self reflected back to him. Unable to make himself in reality, he projects himself as an illusion, though the awareness of his illusoriness drives him to seek the other extreme – unconsciousness, sleep, and the return to the womb. He calls his wife, Soledad, his "homeland", his "final earth", and his mother; he wants to bury himself in her. "You will be my tomb ... Oh! if only I could become smaller ... smaller ... a child ... less than a child ... and incarnate again in your womb, Soledad, and sleep there ... forever, forever."[3] Again there are no alternatives to the satanic wish to be God and the desire for annihilation. The character cannot emerge from his solipsistic fantasy; outside the womb he finds only the ghost of himself posturing on a stage before an imaginary public.

If in these plays Unamuno contrasted acting and dreaming (or sleeping), in others he used them as interchangeable images of self-invention. Towards the end of *El hermano Juan* (the full title is *Brother Juan or the World is Theater*), the hero says, "does Don Miguel de Unamuno exist? Is not everything a misty dream? ... one should not ask if a legendary character existed but only if he exists, if he acts. And Don Juan, Don Quijote and Don Miguel and Segismundo and Don Alvaro and you exist and even I exist ... that is, I dream ... and all those who are seeing and hearing us exist as long as they do so, as long as they dream." In this play, and in its prologue, the dream analogy serves the same function as the theory of play-acting – a defensive screen against his own duplicity, an elaborate double deceit. For if reality and fiction are indistinguishable ("what difference does it make to assert that everything is fiction or that everything is real?"), a life dedicated to the fabrication of one's picture in the minds of others can be characterized as an authentic and historical existence. Wanting to be remembered by others can be transposed into wanting to be remembered

[2] See Iris Zavala, *Unamuno y su teatro de conciencia* (Salamanca: *Acta Salmanticensia*, Filosofía y Letras, I, 1963), p. 15.

[3] Carlos Blanco Aguinaga does not see this kind of sleep as a regressive fantasy of death; instead he describes it as the "good dream" of the contemplative Unamuno (*El Unamuno contemplativo*, p. 135) and, referring to *Soledad*, he identifies it with "the idea of the mother as a living image of the subconscious" (p. 137). Iris Zavala, on the other hand, stresses what she sees as the play's ontological message – life is representation and man is the creature who makes himself (op. cit., p. 163). Yet this vision of self-creation is treated in the play as both satanic arrogance (650) and a delusion that can be cured only by the disintegration of the ego in the maternal womb and tomb.

by God. And vanity, which makes one give oneself to the gaze of others in order "to be admired, to be seen, and to leave a name" can become "the struggle for life"; it can be dignified as the "spiritual need to portray and thereby make oneself eternal . . . in the theater that is the history of Humanity".

But the actor who fashions his mask for the sake of his public depends on it totally and the awareness of that dependence can destroy his faith in the value of the performance. In the prologue Unamuno says that Don Juan is always "provoking others to dream their dreams of him"; he is the dream of the women he seduces and he dreams his own dream of himself in them. In other words, he is, as he himself confesses, "their creation", and the knowledge that he owes his existence to others, that he is almost entirely imaginary, makes him long for his own destruction; he looks forward to death which he thinks of as both mother and bride to whose dark womb ("dug out with his own hands") he will return – "voy a casa, a casarme." The prologue's hopeful vision of eternal life won in the theater of history is negated by Juan's final despairing farewell to the stage.

Niebla too shows – in some ways contrary to the author's expressed intentions – the hazards of maintaining one's existence through fantasy. Augusto Pérez discovers, to his great humiliation, that he, who has spent his life dreaming private dreams and has even succeeded in inventing an imaginary fiancée, is the invention of one Miguel de Unamuno. As Antonio Machado said in *Juan de Mairena*, if I convert the other into a figment of my imagination, he is apt to repay me in kind. "Life is a dream" may mean that someone else is dreaming us; the dream becomes a symbol of self-estrangement.

Unamuno, however, repeatedly affirms the contrary. "Life may be a dream, but I who dream it am not a dream." He is in control after all. He would like to think that dreaming means fashioning his own destiny. Dreamers, like actors, create themselves – they are people of "substance". In his Canary Island exile he wrote that the men who sent him there were nothing but his dreams. "I dream them . . . they, for their part, do not dream, they are incapable of dreaming."[4] Only the dreamer can be an autonomous creator. "He will choose himself resolutely imaginary so as to derive from himself alone."[5] Man even creates God by dreaming of Him, by wanting to believe in Him. And God, in turn, creates man and dreams the universe – Unamuno wonders if the world would disappear if God were to stop dreaming it (XVI, 358) and he often said that we offer hymns and prayers to God to keep him asleep and dreaming of us. God and man are locked in a mutually sustaining dream. In the prologue to 1935 edition of *Niebla* he says that immortality, like the dream, is either communal or it is nothing; the "grandiose illusion" (*ensueño*, one of the variants of of *sueño*) of apocatastasis is collective salvation. From this kind of connection between dreaming and immortality Unamuno moves to their identification – the dream of immortality *is* immortality. Unamuno turns Calderón upside down. "This is the mist, the *nivola*, the legend, this is eternal life . . . and this is the creative, dreaming word".

Novel, theater, and dream become in his works interchangeable symbols and

---

[4] Quoted by Zubizarreta, *Unamuno en su nivola*, p. 40.
[5] Sartre describes Genet's strategy thus; Sartre, *St. Genet*, p. 389.

each one of them can be used to describe either the ideal of a "substantial" and eternal reality or the despairing vision of insecurity and hallucination. Unamuno shifts back and forth between negative and positive connotations and continually alters the emotional charge of his metaphors. He might in the same book – on the same page – evoke the nostalgia for mystical dream and argue the need to wake people up to anguish and spiritual torment (XVI, 405). Thus, the most negative vision of sleep as annihilation can, with the twist of a word, reveal itself as the dream of eternity and substance. And what Unamuno called the most terrifying variation on the theme – Shakespeare's "we are such stuff as dreams are made on" – might be reversed to show that perhaps the "stuff" (Unamuno translates it *madera*, "wood", derived from *materia*) is substantial and persistent. "Could we not say that dreams are made of the same stuff that we touch and feel in our spiritual entrails?" (III, 766). Statements abound whose meaning transforms itself before our eyes; his language becomes an iridescent shimmer in which different planes and levels of reality and unreality slide across each other and from which the most contrary messages may be extracted.[6] One can never be sure if the total fictitiousness of the universe is meant to console or bring disillusion. In his late works Unamuno moved ever closer to that "hypnotic sense of life" of which he spoke so scornfully in "Plenitud". But we feel that he is sleepwalking and that he could at any moment awaken to the realization that dreams are nothing but dreams – "los sueños, sueños son".

---

[6] Unamuno's usage reminds us of the "antithetical meaning of primal words" that Freud related to ambivalence of feeling.

PART TWO
FICTION

Introduction

All Gods and all masters!
(Del sentimiento trágico de la vida)

All of Unamuno's fictions are strongly dualistic. Many are built on paired contraries, the characters representing polarities or the split halves of a single whole whose differences are heightened and exaggerated during the course of the narrative. In other works the antagonist is drawn out of the soul of the protagonist; he is a double, a projected but phantasmal self. The central theme of illusion vs. reality is invariably posed in terms of conflict. But the oppositional scheme is countered by diverse attempts, on the level of characterization, plot, or symbolic imagery, to overcome the split, either by violent appropriation and the destruction of the antagonist or by the immersion of the historical world into a fictitious one. The first appears in the characters' impulse towards fixity (as the hero of *El otro* says, the aim is to be "one, always one and the same") which makes for a simple plot structure of duplicating and unresolved tension. The other unifying effort is evident in the author's metaphorical transformation of reality into fiction. The dramatic conflict ends therefore either in the isolation and destruction of the characters or in a dream of a fictional universe shared by both author and characters.

The novels are all basically power struggles. The satanic formula "all or nothing" makes the characters strive for a god-like self-sufficiency; they are consumed by enormous ambition. Even in those who seem to be self-abnegating, meek, muddled, or evasive (Angela and Don Manuel in *San Manuel Bueno*, Berta in *Dos madres*, Augusto Pérez in *Niebla*, the narrator of "Don Sandalio") we discover the traces of a hidden pride and a secret envy of God's power and autonomy. In the novels and plays where those passions are explicitly presented as motivating impulses of the plot (*Abel Sánchez*, *Tres novelas ejemplares*, *La tía Tula*, *El otro*), the characters act like people in the grip of demonic forces they can neither control nor comprehend. All their actions are fated. Unamuno's characters, contrary to what is often said about them (by critics who read into them Unamuno's many statements about the will to self-creation), live in a realm of total unfreedom; their lust for dominion is the measure of their subjugation. He who would possess all others is himself a man possessed.[1]

---

[1] Those critics who do see the characters' lack of freedom attribute it to Unamuno's unwillingness to let them develop according to their own laws. See Agnes Moncy, "La creación del personaje en las novelas de Unamuno", *La Torre*, 9 (Puerto Rico 1963), pp. 145-88; Francisco Ayala, "El arte de novelar en Unamuno", in his *Realidad y*

Other novels (*Niebla*, "Don Sandalio", *San Manuel Bueno*) weave around the unrevealed secrets of arrogance and envy a web of confusions, a "mist" of doubt and delusion. Both characters and author argue that truth and deception, reality and fiction, are indistinguishable. If in *Cómo se hace una novela*, this argument is limited to its assertive formulation, in works like *Niebla* and "Don Sandalio" it becomes entangled in a narrative network that almost, but not entirely, achieves the autonomy of fiction. Because all of Unamuno's novels and plays stress the personal "message" (Unamuno said that "no one tells a story with no other end in mind but telling a story", XVI, 569), they are schematic and allegorical;[2] when successful they stand as objective and exemplary moral tales; when unsuccessful they remain within the private world of the author's contradictory affirmations.

The stark formulas of the fiction are eloquently rendered through the simplicity and bareness of Unamuno's most characteristic narrative manner. After *Paz en la guerra* (1897), he abandoned the formal features of realistic or mimetic fiction – wealth of detail, explicit development of the relation between the social-historical context and the inner life of the characters, visual descriptions of both characters and scene, authorial interpretation of motivation and action. *Amor y pedagogía* (1902), his second novel, marks a radical departure from the first and contains what Unamuno described as the germ of the other novels; it combines a story that is both melodramatic and comical with a running philosophical commentary. I shall not examine these first two works but concentrate on those that follow them.

In *Niebla* (1914) Unamuno develops his personal version of the novelistic genre (what he called the *nivola*). Except for *Paz en la guerra* it is his longest novel, but consists almost entirely of dialogue and monologue. Its several subordinate anecdotes are like exemplary tales that mirror or prefigure parts of the main plot. The setting, a provincial city, exists mainly in and through the protagonist's occasional and fragmented awareness of the world outside himself; social reality manifests itself almost entirely in the subjective responses of the character.

The novels that follow *Niebla* are all close to drama in the reliance on dialogue and in the rapid development of plot. At times the text reproduces the conventions of the written play where speeches are preceded only by the speaker's name. There is little structural difference between a novella like *Dos madres* (1920) and the play *El otro* (1926). The narrator (usually an omniscient third person) limits his descriptions of thoughts and feelings to a few brief metaphorical insertions in the rapid course of the action. In the prologue to *Tres novelas ejemplares* (1920), Unamuno argued against a "realism" that offers only the stage setting, décor, costume, landscape. "The figures of the realists are usually dressed-up mannikins that move around on a string and have inside them a phonograph which repeats the phrases their Maese Pedro has picked up in streets and plazas" (IX, 415). He proposes to set before the reader a reality

---

ensueño (Madrid: Gredos, 1963); Manuel Durán, "La técnica de la novela y la generación del 98", *Revista Hispánica Moderna*, 23 (1957), pp. 14-27.
[2] Angus Fletcher's approach to allegory casts much light on Unamuno's fictions. *Allegory: The Theory of a Symbolic Mode* (Ithaca: Cornell University Press, 1964).

that is "inner, creative, a thing of will". He wants to reveal the true self of the character, not the external and false one, and he reminds us again by way of reference to the theory of the four Juans that the true self is the one a person wants to be. Although this theory makes, as we shall see, for a certain ambiguity in the presentation of character, it also has significant effects on other aspects of novelistic technique. Unamuno wants to create what he sees as a new fictional form (the *nivola*) that does not allow description, character analysis or plot complication to interfere with the swift uncovering of the essential "inner" process – the clash of wills. Little time is wasted in the evocation of a densely populated human world or in any reconstruction of the characters' past; the narrative opens immediately onto a conflict of passions that moves quickly and inexorably to a disastrous conclusion.

Unamuno conscientiously excluded anything but the barest descriptions of scene from most of his fictions after *Paz en la guerra*. Although the setting is usually urban, he drastically limits the number of his characters, pulling only a few out of the city crowd. Their struggles for domination sometimes illumine the hierarchical structure of society, but that structure is not in itself an object of novelistic attention; the characters use the social situation as one weapon among others. Unamuno's love of landscape found expression in non-fictional reportage and the lyrical descriptions of books like *Visiones y andanzas* and *Por tierras de Portugal y España,* but the novelistic dramas play themselves out indoors, far from nature. Psychological enclosure is matched by physical enclosure. When the rural landscape does reappear – in "Don Sandalio" and *San Manuel Bueno* – in the form of a few carefully selected and symbolic elements, it serves as a costuming for the protagonist, a metonymical expression of personal traits. Throughout his fiction, Unamuno remains faithful to his claim for the superior reality of the inner world.

I

Masters and Slaves

Dos madres, Nada menos que todo un hombre (1920) and *La tía Tula* (1921) dramatize different aspects of a theme first developed in *Amor y pedagogía* and present in some way in all of Unamuno's fictions – creation of another or of others. They are stories about spiritual, as opposed to physical, paternity or maternity. This theme in turn embodies another one – the dream of self-creation and total control. The novelist seeks to fabricate a counter-world in the pages of the novel, a world in which he can, as Unamuno said in *Cómo se hace una novela*, "create himself", and the characters attempt to do the same in the "real" world of their fictions. They attempt to fill an inner void by appropriating the being of someone who is either rival or lover. But a captured subjectivity is no subjectivity at all; it cannot give the confirmation the captor needs. The effort to create the self by devouring others is doomed to failure, destroying both the one who devours and the one who is devoured.

These conflicts have been compared to Hegel's account of the struggle between the master and the slave.[1] The parallels are striking. As in Hegel's account, the master inevitably ends up in a position of dependence because he needs the slave for the recognition of himself as master. "Just where the master has effectively achieved lordship, he really finds that something has come about quite different from an independent consciousness. It is not an independent but rather a dependent consciousness that he has achieved."[2] But whereas Hegel goes on to show how, in certain respects, the slave has the advantage over the master, Unamuno's stories end at the moment of the master's failure, at that point where he finds himself alone, without the others whose recognition he seeks. Unamuno's fictions are about reversals in a struggle for control that, unlike the Hegelian dialectic, is potentially endless (though sometimes, as we shall see, Unamuno intervenes to impose his own version of reconciliation).

The theme lends itself to a symmetrical patterning of reversible motifs and narrative structures. The characters are drawn as contraries or duplicates so that their relationships are mirrored as one plays the role of the other. Thus in *Dos madres* (IX, 424-55) an erotic triangle emerges through the self-assertive drive of one of the characters, the widow Raquel (mistress of Juan), but Unamuno carefully shows how her counterpart and rival, the innocent young Berta, adopts the same aims and projects. Berta imitates Raquel and her love is

---

[1] Carlos Blanco Aguinaga, "Aspectos dialécticos de las *Tres novelas ejemplares*", *Revista de Occidente*, 19 (1964), pp. 51-70.
[2] *The Phenomenology of Spirit*, trans. James Baillie (London: Allen and Unwin, 1931), pp. 236-7.

an imitated love. The rival is also a model; in fact the rivalry springs from an imitation of another's desire.[3]

The competition between Berta and Raquel is, of course, founded upon a reversal in the traditional relations of dominance between male and female. In almost all of Unamuno's fictions the woman pursues and the man is the passive, even abject, object of pursuit. Don Juan is the trophy disputed by the two women; he finds himself torn between "two mothers". The pursuing woman is also a mother ready to destroy the child in order to affirm her rights of possession ("he felt like the child brought before Solomon . . . only he did not know which one of them . . . wanted him whole for the other and which wanted to cut him in two").[4] The question of control is not limited to the emotional sphere; as Raquel becomes Juan's "master" she also gets hold of his fortune and later of Berta's as well. Property relations neatly parallel emotional ones.

The novella's opening words are "How Raquel weighed on poor Don Juan!" From the beginning we are told that her love "tastes of death" and that she seeks in her lover something so deep it is "beyond life". Though Don Juan was once, we learn, deserving of his name, he has lost all will and desire and now lives "absorbed" by Raquel, "lost in the widow and her widowhood. . . . 'This woman will kill me.' " He thinks about a sweet eternal rest when he will be covered by the earth, after being killed by "a widow like that". The woman's desire annihilates the man who, for his part, compliantly participates in his own destruction.

While Juan dreams of death, Raquel pursues life, or "something beyond life"; she wants to perpetuate herself in the flesh of another. Since she is barren, she arranges a marriage to produce a child for her. It is Raquel who chooses Berta as the future mother of "her" child ("whether she wants it or not, I want it"). Although he has no "appetite for paternity", Juan obediently courts Berta. The girl is flattered and intrigued with the possibility of "redeeming" the former Don Juan. She is also fascinated with Raquel; in fact her desire for Juan is heightened by her fascination with the woman she knows has been his mistress. She wants to "seize that man from her and see what he is like, the man she has made, the man who has surrendered body and soul . . . What she must have taught him! What my poor Juan must know! . . . And he will make me like her." Unamuno is explicit about the attractive force of the rival. The triangle is welded together by a passion that encompasses both the rival and the disputed male, who is less the object of desire than the rival herself. It is the rival who confers value on the loved one (as René Girard says, "the impulse toward the object is ultimately an impulse toward the mediator", and, quoting the Proustian narrator, "in love, our successful rival . . . is our benefactor. To a person who aroused in us only an insignificant physical desire, he adds an immense prestige

[3] This is the pattern of mediated or triangular desire analysed so well by René Girard in *Deceit, Desire, and the Novel*, trans. Yvonne Freccero (Baltimore: The Johns Hopkins Press, 1965).
[4] In order to keep track of the contradictory statements and arguments in Unamuno's essays, I give page references throughout. I do not think this is necessary in the case of the fiction and so, for the sake of an uninterrupted text, I omit them. I have used both the Afrodisio Aguado and Escelicer editions of the *Obras completas*.

and value").[5] Juan is the lure which draws Berta to Raquel. "The person Berta was madly in love with was Raquel. Raquel was her idol." Unamuno shows both the fascination of the rival and her god-like power. Juan tells Raquel, "she is madly in love with you – you have subjugated her".

Yet the compliance in subjugation is a means to ultimate dominion; Berta identifies with Raquel, fuses with her in order to steal the secret of her power. She studies the older woman to find out "how to win over her husband and win herself, to be like Raquel, to be a woman". And so she let herself be "absorbed by Juan's master and she began to discover herself through the other". Being a woman means possessing both the man and the other woman, incorporating both into the substance of her being. In what might be described as an involution of the maternal theme, Berta submits to the rival in the hope of giving birth to herself.

Raquel fully understands this; knowing that the girl observes and copies her, she hopes that passion will, as she says, bear fruit. Raquel clearly thinks of herself as the "father" of Berta's child; the union of Raquel's will and Berta's desire must fructify. The homoeroticism of Berta's infatuation never becomes a part of the story because Unamuno is much less concerned with the external expression of sexuality than with the hidden drama of conquest and surrender – and envy – in which they are anchored. It is Raquel's power that compellingly attracts the girl; the widow seems to incarnate an absolute control that entrances the others. Just as Juan cannot help but admire the force that has destroyed him, Berta cannot help but covet it. In both cases, the illusion of autonomy proves irresistible.

The woman's desire signifies enslavement or dispossession. "Why have you captivated me?" Juan asks Raquel, "why have you sucked the marrow of my will? . . . Am I mine? Am I myself? Why have you stolen my body and soul?" Such total and devastating ownership is, in the world of this story, the maternal tie. To Juan's anguished questions Raquel replies, "why should I want any child but you?" Both "mothers" are ready to tear the child apart. Although he refers to Berta as his "redeeming angel" and to Raquel as his "redeeming demon" each one (fair maid and femme fatale) is as deadly as the other; both represent the abyss. "The clear blue eyes of Berta, the virgin, like a bottomless, shoreless sea, called him to the abyss, and behind him . . . enveloping him, the black shadowy eyes of Raquel, the widow, like a bottomless, starless night, pushed him towards the same abyss." The woman does not give birth to the child but sucks him in and drowns him in a bottomless sea. The sea was always for Unamuno the maternal element and although he often connected it with eternity and mystical union, we see here that the positive and negative associations (sea and night) fuse into the latter – the terror of annihilation.[6] *Dos madres* is about the destructiveness of motherhood.

Yet the story begins with Raquel's sterility; the plot is engendered by her decision to overcome it by sheer force of will. She is obsessed with the power of

---

[5] Girard, p. 24.

[6] Blanco Aguinaga has carefully traced the positive and negative associations of the water symbol in Unamuno's works (*El Unamuno contemplativo*). Here we see their secret unity.

creation. For her the inability to create is the measure of human nothingness and hell is "the center of a sterile womb". Creation, in this novella, is synonymous with dominion. Emptiness is powerlessness. In order not to be "nothing", Unamuno said we must strive to be everything. The theme of creation easily transforms itself into the desperate urge to be everything, the urge to constitute oneself as God. What Raquel seeks is a divine self-sufficiency. Like God, she wants to find the mirror of herself in her creation : her child – or her lover – should reflect back her own image. When Juan tells her that his wife is pregnant, she "gazed at herself in the pupils of his eyes, at the tiny image of herself . . . she gazed fixedly at her own miniature portrait reflected in his eyes and then, as if out of her senses, she murmured in a hoarse voice, 'let me kiss myself', and she covered his eyes with kisses". The scene is repeated several times. She must have been seeking in Juan a desire capable of arousing or heightening her own self-directed passion. Raquel bewitches the other so that she may draw from his (or her) eyes the image of her own desirable self. It is ultimately reunion with herself that she aims at but she needs the mediation of the other.

This need, however, shows her own insufficiency. Without the other she cannot see herself. The desire for perfect autonomy leads to dependence on the mediator. In Berta's view, Raquel is omnipotent but her power turns out to be illusory. Although the novella ends with her apparent triumph – Juan is killed in an accident that is possibly a suicide, and Raquel is left in control of Berta's child, Berta's money, and her future – one suspects that the destructive cycle of her love will play itself out again with the child ("my Quelina, who is I myself"). In *Del sentimiento trágico* Unamuno preached an ethic of mutual imposition ("each one nourishes himself with the flesh of the one he devours") and described love as the effort to exist in and through the other. In *Dos madres* that love negates the free subjectivity of the beloved.

At one point the story links the character's obsessive need for motherhood with the theme of revenge. Juan feels that he is no more than an instrument. "For what? For satisfying a gnawing hunger for motherhood? Or rather, a strange vengeance, a vengeance of other worlds." In the first paragraph we read that Juan and Raquel lived in their illegitimate and solitary home like two lovers in a monastic cell and, since we remember that Unamuno often called the monastery the incubator of pride and envy, we might suspect that Raquel's lust for power is a vindictive assault on the source of all power and creation. Raquel, like Dr. Montarco, envies God himself.

Title, names, and situations refer us to the Book of Genesis (the stories of Rachel, Sara, Rebecca, and of Agar and Lea) but we can also see the characters' struggles as demonic efforts to steal the secret of God's power. The theme of self-creation leads to a debased version of the story of the Fall. The language of the characters suggests that they conceive of their plight in terms of a cosmic drama; they see their dependence as sign of a fallen state. Thus when Juan talks about "redemption", he is thinking of release from his bondage to Raquel. And all of them (Raquel, Juan, Berta's parents and Berta herself) refer to the girl as the "redeemer" who will liberate Juan from his captivity. But the "angelic creature" is herself so enthralled that she cannot distinguish between his redemption and her own ("she was eager for Don Juan's redemption. For Don Juan's or her own?"). Yet thralldom is nothing other than a covetous fascination with power. This would seem to be the original and ineradicable sin. In dreaming of salvation, Berta is trapped by her own ambition. By the dynamic of "all or nothing" the desire for redemption easily passes over into boundless desire; the slave wants not only freedom but lordship as well. For Berta redemption comes to mean dominion – she wants to be like Raquel, like her "idol". When she realizes she has been duped, she recognizes the enormity of her aspiration; she had let herself be "tempted by the serpent to taste the fruit of the Tree of Knowledge of good and evil". The autonomy that Raquel and Berta aim at is total – and therefore impossible.

In the Prologue to *Tres novelas ejemplares y un prólogo*, Unamuno makes an invidious comparison between "literary" art and "poetic" or "creative" art. *Dos madres* tells the story of a "creative" or maternal impulse that leads to subjugation, death, and solitude. The implications of this for the artist's own creativity are not explored here although the complexities of the relation between author and character constituted a central theme in *Niebla*, written six years earlier, and the same topic reappears, in disguised form, thirteen years later in "Don Sandalio, jugador de ajedrez". Nor does Unamuno deal with the contradictions between the prologue and the fictional works that supposedly exemplify its principles. The novels of what we might call a middle period (from *Abel Sánchez*, 1917, to *La tía Tula*, 1921) represent a temporary abandonment of the explicit treatment of novelistic creativity which, in earlier and later works, finds expression in the conscious manipulation of the shifting frontiers of reality and fiction.

*   *   *

In *Nada menos que todo un hombre* ("Nothing Less Than a Real Man", IX, 472-518) the theme of domination is elaborated through a dual, not triangular, situation. But since Unamuno's triangles invariably reveal a power struggle between alternating pairs within the triangle, this plot simply strips the conflict of desire to its most basic structure. The "third person" ("el otro") who does appear is quite clearly used as a pawn by the two primary characters, each one of whom seeks to affirm an independent sense of self through and against the other. The cultural context of the drama is succinctly and forcefully established; both antagonists reflect a specific social and economic situation that reduces them (and everyone else) to the status of objects.

All her life Julia Yáñez, the daughter of an impoverished upper-class family has been treated as something that could be bought, sold, or bartered. Famous for her beauty, she is regarded not as a person but a thing, a "monument" (she and the Cathedral are the provincial city's two claims to fame) and her father has long been trying to capitalize on what he calls his "treasure" in order to improve the family position. Alejandro Gómez, who was, as he says, "almost born on a dung heap", made his fortune in the colonies and works hard to prove himself to and in defiance of the aristocracy of Renada. Expressing his disdain for them, he makes a proud display of his plebeian ways; since they would treat him like a nobody if it were not for his money, he must show them that he alone among them is truly independent, deriving from himself alone. He is a

child of his deeds: "You come from illustrious parents and noble families –
I . . . have had neither parents nor any family except the one I have made. I
come from nothing."

Unamuno tells most of the story from the perspective of Julia who is ini-
tially the weaker of the two. Since she is the one most in need of affirmation, she
is attracted by Alejandro's magnificent self-sufficiency, by his way of saying "I".
In all Renada he alone seems to have an autonomous subjectivity (the name of
the city suggests "reino de la nada", a kingdom of nothingness). "Every time
Alejandro said 'I' she would tremble. She trembled with love although she
thought it was for some other reason, or else was totally ignorant of its cause."
Part of that unknown cause must be the wish to link herself with the man who
lives like a god in the radiance of his own being. She looks upon him as a potential "redeemer".

Unamuno does not explain the motivations of his characters. The reader is
given only intense but laconic dialogue and extremely summary descriptions of
feeling. When Alejandro writes to Julia that she will eventually be his, because
Alejandro Gómez knows how to get what he wants, she thinks, "Here is a real
man. Will he save me? Or will I save him?" A page or so later, "She was conquered. And so the wedding was arranged".

Most of the narrative tells of Julia's self-tormenting passion for her husband:
"unwilling to love him, she felt herself yielding to a submission that was a kind
of love . . . something like the love an arrogant conqueror must inspire in the
heart of his captive." Alejandro requires that she accept the status of a possession, that she let herself be used and displayed like "a tamed lion". Gradually
she develops "the soul of a slave-girl in a harem". Her fascination and subjugation grow hand in hand with incomprehension. Both the feelings of her "lord
and master" and her own reactions to him seem increasingly opaque to her, and
the narrator does not elucidate them ("as time went on she understood her
husband less and less and felt more and more subjugated"). But one might
guess that the slave complies in her humiliation in order to share in the conqueror's power; she can thus identify her will with his, take his being into
her own. Her abasement is inseparable from the imagined pleasure of his arrogant disdain. Humiliation turns out to be a round-about route to dominion. In
Del sentimiento trágico Unamuno says "being conquered, or at least appearing
to be so, is often the same as conquering; taking what is the other's is a way of
living in him" (XVI, 407).[7]

Yet the plot centers on Julia's increasingly imperative wish for evidence of her
husband's love. Over and over she asks if he loves her, and resolutely he refuses
to talk about such foolish and "novelistic" things. When she tries to arouse his
jealousy with a young aristocrat, Alejandro denies that she could feel anything
but what he wills her to feel. "I know you could not love another . . . even if you
tried to do so." Therefore, of course, she can see her little "kitten" as often as she
wants – she is completely free. Free, yet not free. Free, but the incarnation of
his will. These contrary assertions drive her to despair. When she confesses

---

[7] "The masochist is a revolutionist of self-surrender . . . His yielding includes defiance,
his submissiveness opposition." Theodor Reik, *Masochism and Modern Man* (New York:
Farrar, Straus), p. 156.

adultery to him he has her committed to an insane asylum. And when she returns and asks forgiveness he says that since the wife of Alejandro Gómez can do no wrong, she needs no forgiveness. Not for a moment does he permit her the autonomy of the slightest offense. His power and her subjection are total. She looks at him with a "mad love . . . a blind love fused with an equally blind terror".

In Hegel the struggle between master and slave moves in a spiralling reversal. Although the slave turns out to get, in a way, the better of the master, the story does not end there because that combat was the starting point of the evolution of self-consciousness. In Unamuno's fictions the reversal is always complete and perfectly balanced; nothing is surpassed because roles are simply exchanged. In this text the exchange is signaled by an abrupt alteration in the character of Alejandro. Suddenly, the narrator tells us, he reveals to his wife "the depths of that terrible and hermetic soul", and she sees "the black and shadowy lake of that soul". He bursts out with the confession that he loves her more than his own self, that he is hers more than she is his – that she is his "goddess", his "all". And at this point Julia says she would like to die.

That wish is slowly realized, though Alejandro tries frantically to save her. His desperation fills her with "the sweetest light. How happy she was at last!" Hers was a "sad joy of triumph". He is nothing but her man, "the one you have made me!" She dies and he kills himself. The effort to create the self by absorbing the other ends in mutual annihilation. "Each one nourishes himself with the flesh of the one he devours."

As in *Dos madres,* the characters see their lives in cosmic terms; she thinks of him as the "redeemer" and he calls her his goddess" though, contrary to what happens in the first novella, Unamuno does not here develop the theme of a degraded religious drama and even seems to be unaware of it. Since each treats the other only through this exalted fantasy, neither one has anything to do with the real presence of the other. Those who make gods of each other renounce human existence. The wish to be God is the wish not to be oneself. "The affirmation of the self ends in the negation of the self. The will to be God is a will to self-destruction which is gradually realized" (Girard, 228). Aspiring to be all, one ends up being nothing.

Yet Unamuno does not see his fiction in these terms. The melodramatic conclusion is presented in all seriousness. The lovers cherish their passion precisely because it destroys them – the fulfillment of love consumes the self. It is a "magnificent and desirable disaster", to use Denis de Rougemont's phrase for the self-inflaming, self-directed passion he has described so well.[8] At the end it is Alejandro who speaks of subjugation; " 'Yours, yours, yours, only yours, and nothing but yours' he used to whisper to her, while she, clinging to his neck, would almost strangle him with her embrace". For Unamuno wanting to die and wanting to kill are the expression of true love. Death in love is transfiguration. Annihilation is redemption. At the story's end, Unamuno clearly shares the values of his characters. Years later, in the prologue to *El hermano Juan,* he fondly recalled them, saying that Alejandro was a tyrant out of timidity (we

[8] *Love in the Western World* (New York: Doubleday Anchor, 1957), p. 11.

might ask if by the same token his final self-abnegation means he has become truly tyrannical).

The lack of distance between author and characters helps explain the fact that Alejandro's transformation is both surprising and unconvincing. Although we have seen often enough in the essays that a defiantly maintained isolation calls up the reactive yearning to lose oneself in the other, Unamuno does not develop this connection in the narrative; he gives us such a limited and restricted view of Alejandro that the reversal seems gratuitous – it makes sense only in the light of mechanisms observed in Unamuno's essays. And since Unamuno was often unaware of those mechanisms, he does not here make them part of the fiction. As for Julia, in the same prologue, Unamuno says she died happy because her "death is love as love is death", a statement that must be related to Unamuno's view that love is pain and that pain is man's greatest good. The end of *Nada menos que todo un hombre* is melodramatic because there is no deviation in perspective between the characters and author; all share a highly eroticized vision of death as self-consummation.[9]

In this work, Unamuno's control of his fictional material is questionable; he works against the very situation he has created. From the objective description of lordship and bondage in the first part, he moves to an authorial underwriting of the character's aims. Thus, although this novel shows as clearly as *Dos madres* the devastating consequences of those aims, the ending denies the truth of that negative vision. This reminds us of the crucial equivocations of Unamuno's essays – emptiness is fulness, being is the longing to be, external appearances constitute the true inner substance, hypocrisy is sincerity, and dreams are the real stuff of life. In the essays, oppositions are usually neither surpassed, reconciled, nor even recognized, but systematically confused in the surface of language; in *Nada menos que todo un hombre* they are merged in the final turn of the plot. Fiction gives way to a kind of morbid fantasy in which the most negative desires are presented as the highest spiritual achievement. "Love is death as death is love."

*   *   *

[9] The novel's critics do not question this idealization of destructive love. R. Gullón says that Julia's love is a "pure flame . . . which melts the ice of pride" and that she dies because she "has worn herself out in the task of creating love and security" (op. cit., 191-2), C. Blanco Aguinaga argues that "the novel's ending describes the last moment of the dialectical process . . . man and wife recognize each other and know each other . . . Both are authors and creatures; Subjects in communion, no longer Objects, instruments, things. Total consciousness in union but at death's door, in death." In asserting that the ending is necessarily tragic because "harmony, the definitive synthesis" is not possible in "history itself", he glosses over the novel's presentation of death as itself union ("Aspectos dialécticos . . .", pp. 66-7). Others see an existential allegory: for Angel del Río, Alejandro embodies "man's will deprived of spiritual strength . . . the inscrutable designs of God . . . give him tragic dimensions" and the novel shows that "we are condemned to live in agony" (Introduction, *Three Exemplary Novels*, trans. Angel Flores, New York: Grove Press, 1956, p. 33); Segundo Serrano Poncela says he personifies the "force of will" which is "crushed by the gratuity of life" (*El pensamiento de Miguel de Unamuno*, Mexico: Fondo de Cultura Económica, 1953, p. 185). But neither the inscrutable designs of God nor the absurdity of existence account for Alejandro's tragedy; he himself is responsible.

In the prologue to *La tía Tula* (*Aunt Tula*, 1921, IX, 521-634) Unamuno compared the novel to *Abel Sánchez* because both delve into the dark "cellars and hiding places of the heart, catacombs of the soul". The readers who found that novel inhuman will find this one so also, he says. *Abel Sánchez* is about "fraternal" relations – and Unamuno reminds us that the first fraternal act was Cain's – and *La tía Tula* is about "sororal" ones. For Unamuno the sibling tie invariably suggests two linked themes – psychological splitting and the goal of total self-sufficiency that lies behind it. *La tía Tula* focuses on the second, though aspects of the first are naturally a part of the protagonist's characterization.

The novel opens with contrasting portraits of two sisters, Rosa and Gertrudis (Tula) who are, Unamuno says, like two halves of a sundered whole. This initial opposition sets up a physical and psychological duality that will be resolved by the destruction or absorption of one by the other. Unamuno's description evokes the dichotomy of inner and outer, spirit and flesh: Rosa opens to the world "the flower of her flesh", whereas Tula is like "a locked and sealed coffer in which one divines a treasure of tenderness and secret pleasure". Rosa's beauty attracts but Tula's "tenacious eyes" capture. If Gertrudis represents the invisible inner substance (the inner self), the novel, on one level, dramatizes the war between body and soul as the protagonist tries to affirm her spirit and assure its continuity through the creation of new beings. Like Raquel, Tula aims at a purely spiritual maternity.

Her characterization is wholly in terms of the exaltation of spirit over matter; she hates sensuality; she hates the flesh. Because she would like to be a disembodied will, she scrupulously avoids any compromise with the body. When Rosa's suitor, Ramiro, begins to notice her, she quickly arranges a marriage that will free her for what she describes as her vocation to be an aunt, that is, a spiritual mother.[10] Like Raquel, Tula uses another to conceive and bear for her so that the child can be the uncontaminated offspring of her will. Although she is, as Unamuno says, "all soul", she seeks incarnation in another as if her spirit were trying, in a circuitous way, to reunite itself with the body through the creation of a child who would be, in spite of its real parentage, hers. This "spiritual maternity" entails, of course, a complete disregard for the physical parents; when Rosa almost dies in childbirth, Tula does not allow the doctor to risk the child's life in order to save the mother who, being flesh and not spirit, is dispensable.

The plot is linear and simple, tracing Tula's ever-growing control over her sister's household and the constancy of a virginity that is more than physical. When Rosa dies after the birth of her third child, Ramiro tries to persuade Tula to marry him, but she is repelled by his "brutishness", she esteems herself too highly to serve as the "remedy" for some man's sensuality. Besides, married to Ramiro she would be the stepmother of his children and she prefers to be the "spiritual" mother. "The idea of children of her own flesh made the marrow of her soul's bones tremble with sacred terror, for Gertrudis was all maternity, but spiritual maternity." Ramiro, desiring Tula, gets a servant girl pregnant

---

[10] Helene Deutsch discusses this novel in terms of the cleavage between motherhood and eroticism in *The Psychology of Women*, II (New York: Grune and Stratton, 1944-45), pp. 28-30.

and Tula forces them to marry, thus turning him into her obedient child and reducing the maid to reproductive servitude. The girl bears two children for Tula and dies during her second delivery. Ramiro dies shortly afterwards and Tula is left in undisputed control of a family forged by her will, a "pure" family of innocent children and a virgin mother.

Tula seeks to recreate the home in which she and her sister grew up. Orphaned early, they lived with an uncle, a pious old priest who brought them up "with the cult of the Virgin Mother and the cult of their mother and their grandmother". Her ideal is a succession through parthenogenesis, a community of untainted spirits (women and children) who live free from the flesh and ignorant of it. She wants a chaste home where "no door ever has to be closed, a home without mysteries".

The division of the sexes is, for Tula, a figuration of the struggle between body and spirit – and spirit must triumph since men are "all flesh and very brutish". Yet Tula sees the world teeming with evidence of a frightening and despicable sensuality. During a country vacation, she worries that the sight of farm animals, "serpents in paradise", might corrupt the children. The sea alone appears to be clean, lifeless, sterile, though even the salt air brings a "dangerous tingling". The earth itself is an affront to chastity; she refuses to sit on the ground next to Ramiro and "in front of the children". Purity exists only "in the cell, the cloister, the city". The city, which is a monastery of solitary people, isolates, whereas nature brings them together and couples them. We remember that for Unamuno the monastery is the incubator of envy. Solitude and envy, which are the concomitants of purity, are only hinted at in this novel; they barely emerge as almost hidden themes.

Tula is repelled by life because it is limited and mortal and she longs for absolute dominion. Her idea of virtue is, she says "inhuman", that is, beyond the human. She aims at spiritual impregnability, or rather at the spirit's power to conceive itself. All signs of the body's vulnerability, such as blood and vomit, fill her with "unspeakable disgust", though her need to make the spirit flesh in "her" children leads to copious blood-letting. The novel's gory scenes of childbirth and death, which twice coincide, speak of a fascination that ties together murder and procreation, death and copulation, at once repugnant and alluring. Tula keeps herself free from the flesh by destroying that of others.

Freedom means freedom from all forms of dependence. Tula imagines herself as "an orphan loaded with children", and her passion for maternity excludes any filial feeling ("is this not pride?" she asks). She wants to derive from herself alone, be her own creator and the sole founder of the family (she does not need the collaboration of the male because hers is a spiritual family). The life of the bees intrigues her because their art and tradition, wax and hive, are the work of "aunts" who have no part in the reproductive process. This is the kind of tradition she would like to hand down to "her" children. Yet the need for perfect autonomy means that even the children can exist only as instruments of her will. She calls them her "works", and they themselves come to accept this designation, forgetting their real parents and imagining that they are a "creation of hers". Tula, like Berta and Raquel, would bring forth the world and others in her image.

79

Playing god means the subjection of others; Tula's last years are filled with remorse and self-accusation. She tells her confessor that her life has been "a lie, a mistake, a failure". She charges herself with having used and abused all those around her, for having treated them, as she says on her deathbed, like puppets – "dolls all of them!" At the end she repents of her grandiose and demonic dreams, yet she does not reconcile herself to the human world. She blames herself for rejecting Ramiro and thus precipitating his "fall" into sensuality. Before her death she tells the children, "If you see that someone you love has fallen into a sea of mud – throw yourself in, even at the risk of drowning . . . and if you should die amidst mud and filth? It does not matter . . . we do not have wings – we are not angels . . . we will be in the next life – where there is no mire – no blood!" She veers from the arrogance of total spiritual control to a willed debasement of the flesh. But it is clear that such debasement is really a round-about way of winning control, a self-punishing detour to perfect saintliness; the person who throws himself in the mud earns thereby the right to a purified existence in the next world. In either case she aims at something beyond this world. Tula refuses to live here and with others; to the end she is faithful to her divided vision, longing for the pure world of angels where there is no mire, no blood, no sex.

The rest of the novel describes the family that Tula has founded and the reverence in which her memory is held. The children turn her into the patron saint of a self-contained community, cut off from the society that surrounds it (the lack of references to the outside world heightens the closeted and stifling feel of the novel). The youngest daughter becomes Tula's representative, re-producing her style, gestures, and maxims. Through her, says Unamuno, the "spiritual eternity" of the family was perpetuated. "She had inherited its soul, spiritualized in the Aunt." Since none of the children remembers anything of Tula but her devotion, tenderness, and self-abnegation, the conclusion of the novel seems to signify the fulfillment of her goal – self-duplication. When the youngest says, in the book's final words, that Aunt Tula must forgive and unite them all, it looks as if her life has not been, after all, "a lie, a mistake".

The narrative seems to have shifted gears entirely; one would think that the last pages refer to a different character altogether – Tula as she thought she was and not the rapacious and devouring person revealed by her actions. And there is nothing in the text to indicate that this shift in portrayal is ironic. Unamuno is not contrasting the delusion of the children with the reality of Tula's be-haviour.

This duplicity is not really new, however. The reader might have noticed it earlier when, for example, Unamuno said that Tula was "all maternity, but spiritual maternity", because that phrase, with all the associations the word "spirit" has in his works, takes on a glow of righteousness. He is not there re-ferring to the devastating consequences of the quest for spiritual purity, any more than when he talked about the self that is underneath the self that acts, he was referring to the tormenting dissociation that springs from that concept. As always, Unamuno manages to keep his ideal separate from the violent ges-tures needed to maintain it. The formal characteristics of his novels – rapid development of plot, reduction of description to a bare minimum, highly-charged dialogue that propels events in a swift staccato while giving a sudden, lightning-like illumination to motives and character – facilitate this separation, for they allow him to dramatize the implications of a character's aims and acts without colouring them through the narrator's language. Thus the impressive and almost startling objectivity of his novels frequently conceals Unamuno's contradictory treatment of characters and situations. But then his double-mindedness is revealed, all the more surprisingly, in certain incidental and explanatory comments and, in some novels, in the final turn of the plot. *La tía Tula* first traces the destruction wrought by Tula's passion for purity and control and then redeems that passion in the piety of the conclusion.

In the prologue Unamuno compares Tula to Don Quixote and St. Theresa (in her role of founder of new communities) and contrasts the hazardous competitiveness of "masculine" civilization with the comforting shelter of "feminine" domesticity. If we take these observations as evidence of Unamuno's personal assessment of his character, we might again conclude that he endorses her endeavors. Or does he mean to suggest that just as civilization begins with the murder of the brother, domesticity begins with the murder of the sister? Is he trying to show that good works can be rooted in murderous passions? Yet he seems unaware of the reversal and of the ambivalent presentation of character. The prologue, like the novel itself, presents a puzzling and apparently unrecognized ambiguity that is the textual counterpart of Unamuno's divided aspiration.[11] He does not so much portray the undeniable link between cruelty and kindness (their evolutionary tie in the life of the emotions) as mask the first by the second. The movement is familiar to us from the essays; an impulse becomes its opposite but the author seems to "forget" the connection and presents first one, then the other, as if each were the only reality. The destructiveness of the "creative will," fully exposed in *Dos madres*, is obscured by the wishful endings of *Nada menos que todo un hombre* and *La tía Tula*.

---

[11] It is doubtless this ambivalence and the critics' failure to see it as such that make some interpretations of the novel so bizarre. Carlos Blanco Aguinaga refers to "the kind and tender Aunt Tula" (*El Unamuno contemplativo*, p. 124) and Julián Marías describes it as "the novel of living together"; Tula is a woman whose life "is not destined to nourish itself on itself, but to realize itself in the unity of the home" (op. cit., p. 119); this might tell us more about certain middle class Spanish values than about any abstract ideal of "living together". Ricardo Gullón, on the other hand, does focus on Tula's "predatory instincts" and "the monster hidden behind her abnegation" (op. cit., pp. 209, 214).

II
Mirror Games

Unamuno's repudiation of the external, observable self in favor of the unknown interior self was obviously connected – though he never explicitly described the connection – with the various states of depersonalization reported in the essays. The alienation of the mirror image and the split between consciousness and action made him fear that he was doing just the opposite of what he thought he was doing. The extreme of dissociation is the appearance of the double. If one believes that the body does not represent one's "inner" self, it is only a short step to seeing the body – or the image of the body (the double) – as persecutory and destructive. The external self can become, as Unamuno once said, the murderer of the true self. Although he never recorded any autoscopic experience in his own life, he used it as the subject of a short story, "El que se enterró" ("The Man Who Buried Himself"). *Desdoblamiento* is also the central structural and thematic device of several other works – *Cómo se hace una novela*, "Julio Macedo y Tulio Montalbán," certain stories, and the play, *El otro*. In *Abel Sánchez* doubling is expressed primarily through its invariable accompaniments – self-hate and envy. In *Niebla*, "Don Sandalio", and *San Manuel Bueno* it appears as one aspect of a broader theme, the creation of imaginary persons; those works center on the concept of fiction in order to explore Unamuno's divided feelings about the value of what is made up as opposed to what is merely "real".

"El que se enterró" (1908) is about a young man, Emilio, who has suffered an abrupt change in personality. According to his friends, the once lively and carefree man has become morose, taciturn, and suspicious. He often seems distracted and preoccupied, as if he were far away, in "another world". To one of these friends, the narrator of the story, he explains what has happened. For several months he suffered a vague anxiety and a constant fear of death. One day, when he was alone in his study, a stranger entered and sat down across from him; the man was his exact duplicate. "I felt that the floor gave way beneath me, that the chair disappeared, that the air became thinner; everything I could see, including my other self, slowly dissolved and when I heard the other softly whisper 'Emilio', I felt death. And I died." He awakened to find that he had changed places with the other; his consciousness had passed from his original body which was lying dead on the floor, to its exact reproduction. He had been present at his own death and now faced "the corpse of his past". Since that corpse was real and not metaphorical, he buried it in the garden. He shows his friend the grave and uncovers a part of a skeleton. The narrator says that the character lived out the rest of his life changed in personality but perfectly normal, without giving anyone the slightest reason for thinking him mad.

Since the story, which is very short, does not develop the personality of the protagonist either before or after his encounter with the double, it provides no psychological context for that meeting. Nor does Unamuno construct it in such a way as to suggest connections with other areas of thought and feelings. He does not even exploit the uncanniness of the situation. The story is little more than an outline and seems as unrooted and unexamined as Unamuno's accounts of his own strange experiences before the mirror. Both those descriptions and this story assume that the reader accepts without question events that are presented as more ordinary than extraordinary. Unamuno does not invite speculation since he evidently believes that everyone is prone to episodes of self-estrangement. Anyone might look in the mirror and see himself as someone else. And, just as unremarkably, anyone might meet his double. It is as if the dissociation that gives rise to the phenomenon in the first place also makes for a curious suspension in narrative, whether fiction or non-fiction.

Although Unamuno's later variations on the theme clarify and enrich it, this bare story becomes meaningful when fitted into the general pattern of the literature of the double. There are two basic kinds of doubles in fiction. The first is the division of the self into two incompatible or conflicting parts which may represent the conscious self and the unconscious (or latent) one (E.T.A. Hoffman used the double as the physical embodiment of the unconscious).[1] In some works, such as Henry James's "The Jolly Corner", the double materializes the potentialities the character has never developed; Unamuno called this the "ex-future self". More frequently this double-by-division is the part of the self that is rejected and repressed because of its "base instincts"; a moral self repudiates an immoral one, and the two are projected into two different persons – Dr. Jekyll cannot accept certain aspects of his nature and he fuses them together into a hated and increasingly depraved Hyde (a parallel relation is that between Frankenstein and his monster).[2] Or, as in *The Picture of Dorian Gray,* one self is presented as an artistic, beautiful "dream" that hides the monstrousness of corruptible flesh.

The other type of double is based not on contrast but on duplication. It also originates in internal division, but what is projected onto the opposing self is everything that can be observed by others. Thus the external or empirical self becomes the double of the true inner self. This double threatens the "real" self not because it is so wicked but simply because it denies the "real" self's claim to absolute autonomy. Yet it is precisely that claim that leads to splitting : in its effort to be totally in command, the inner self disowns the visible one which

[1] A. E. Crawly distinguishes between doubles by multiplication and doubles by division, in "Doubles", *Encyclopedia of Religion and Ethics,* ed. James Hastings (London, 1908-26), IV, 853-60. Ralph Tymms, *Doubles in Literary Psychology* (Cambridge, 1949), using the same general categories, refers to the duplicated self and the divided self. For an examination of a much broader range of literary characters, see Robert Rogers, *A Psychoanalytical Study of the Double in Literature* (Detroit: Wayne State University Press, 1970). He incorporates the above terms and makes a further distinction between manifest and latent doubles; the second category includes all types of composite characters.

[2] Masao Miyoshi discusses this parallel in *The Divided Self; A Perspective on the Literature of the Victorians* (New York: New York University Press, 1969), p. 84.

is, after all, committed to the world and subject to the judgments and demands of others. In *The Double*, Dostoyevsky shows very clearly how the protagonist's strange encounter is intimately connected with his secret intention not to be himself. Golyadkin is willing to sacrifice his observable self to the image he has of himself and wishes others to have. Thus, when he meets his supervisor in embarrassing circumstances he wonders if he should recognize the man or pretend "that I am not myself, but somebody else strikingly like me", and he whispers, "I'm all right . . . quite all right. It's not I, it's not I".[3] There is a true self and a false one, the "I" and the "not I", and the two are tied together by shame and rage.[4] "Mr. Golyadkin looked as though he wanted to hide from himself, as though he were trying to run away from himself . . . Mr. Golyadkin did not only want to run away from himself but to be obliterated, to cease to be, to return to dust." The separation between the two reaches its limit when the one wishes the death of the other.

Death and doubling are always closely linked. Just before meeting his double, Golyadkin feels he is "dying, disappearing". Unamuno's Emilio "felt at all hours the invisible presence of death". In many of the writers who have described autoscopic experiences (among others, d'Annunzio, Maupassant, Musset), the fear of death or old age is clearly an important factor.[5] Otto Rank interpreted the transformation of the double idea from an image of the immortal soul in primitive religion to its appearance as the herald of death as evidence of the disintegration of modern personality.[6] But it could be that the very effort to postulate the soul as something consistent and stable is itself a fatal process. The attempt to dissociate from everything that changes, everything that does not meet the impossible demands of the "real" self, is rather hazardous. One cannot really split oneself in two – real me/false me, eternal self/false self – and survive for long.

In double stories, the death of the double usually entails the death of the first self. The destruction of the repudiated self inevitably means the destruction of the "real" self as well. The appearance of the double comes to mean the same thing as death because in both cases the unity and continuity of the ego are destroyed. The fear of the double is the fear of death. Yet in one way the self wants the double, wants to put out there a part of itself; in one way then, it wants its own death. The double is a dream come true, but the dream turns out to be a nightmare. To protect oneself, one kills oneself. In Unamuno's story, the double survives the meeting with the original self but since he is "another",

---

[3] *The Double*, in *Stories of the Double*, ed. Albert J. Guerard (New York: J. B. Lippincott Co., 1967), pp. 62 and 94. *The Double* is from the Constance Garnett translation of *The Eternal Husband and Other Stories*.

[4] Although the split is projected into the "different" personalities of "Golyadkin 1" (who is "honest", "genuine", "real and innocent") and "Golyadkin 2" (who is the "scoundrel", the "sham", "false and worthless"), it is clear that the objective characteristics of each are really indistinguishable from those of the other.

[5] See Lawrence Kohlberg, "Psychological Analysis and Literary Form: A Study of the Doubles in Dostoevsky", *Daedalus*, 92 (1963), pp. 345-62.

[6] "The Double as Immortal Self", *Beyond Psychology* (New York: Dover, 1958), pp. 62-101.

he is not Emilio; the new "Emilio" knows that he has died, that he has, as his friends say, "visited death".

*   *   *

Abel Sánchez (1917) is a novelistic study of the inextricable tie between envy, self-hate, and the lust for fame. It also shows the link between those passions and doubling. In *Del sentimiento trágico de la vida,* Unamuno describes envy (as well as Herostratism) as spiritual hunger and roots it in the desire to persist in the memory of God or of mortals. The need to be seen and remembered motivates the fratricide with which human history begins. Without the other's gaze (in the Biblical account, God's gaze), one is nothing. A sense of radical insufficiency lies at the heart of envy, and from it, Unamuno explains in the prologue to *El hermano Juan,* comes the need to represent oneself and to live in "the theater of world history." By the dynamics of "all or nothing", the envious person strives to obliterate the others (as Dr. Montarco said, we seek to eclipse the fame of others with our own). Yet this vengeful malice is, Unamuno knew very well, directed against the very persons we also secretly revere because they seem to have won the coveted approbation. Envy, as Kirkegaard said (though anyone might have said it), is concealed admiration.[7] It is simultaneously hatred of the other and the desire to be the other, an unbearable fusion of contrary impulses that isolates one from others and from the world. Unamuno says envy is born of solitude, but it would be more accurate to reverse this relation. The one who envies consumes himself in isolation.[8]

In Unamuno's version of the Cain myth, Joaquín and Abel are not brothers but as close as brothers, brought together by their nursemaids in infancy so that "each one came to know himself through the other". This initial conjuction allows us to see their rivalry, which exists from the very beginning, as a kind of doubling. They are at once antagonists and, like Rosa and Tula, the sundered halves of a single whole. Their complementarity is evident in the symmetrical opposition of their personalities (Joaquín gloomy and aloof, Abel affable and well-liked) and of their chosen professions (science and art, though their essential unity is reinforced by a reversal of the standard associations – Joaquín considers his medical science an art and Abel is a dispassionate and "scientific" painter). The competition is presupposed as well as the eventual confusion and fusion of roles and identities.

Since Unamuno feels no need to explain the origin of the rivalry, his story simply traces the intensification of what is presented as a congenital passion. Joaquín, through whose eyes the story is told, says he is predestined, condemned from birth, and the novel's form perfectly reflects this static and fateful vision. *Abel Sánchez* is the first of Unamuno's stark schematic novellas in which the characters' inner torments occupy the whole of the narrative, precluding any complication of structure or characterization. The isolating effects of the pro-

---

[7] *Fear and Trembling, The Sickness unto Death* (New York: Doubleday Anchor 1954), p. 217.

[8] In *Cómo se hace una novela,* Unamuno described envy as "the internal secretion of pride and arrogance", something born of loneliness and self-hate (X, 842-3). He also frequently called it a characteristically Spanish sentiment.

tagonist's obsession are expressed in the bareness of the fictional landscape. There is no elaboration or shading of personality, scene or anecdote. An omniscient narrator limits himself to dialogue and an unadorned record of motivation and feeling, though at certain points he cedes his place to the protagonist's own account in the form of a diary. The narrative can be compared to Joaquín's hatred – "an ice so transparent that everything can be seen through it with perfect clarity". Secondary characters are reduced to the minimum needed to sustain the action, and the adversary, Abel, appears more as the obsessive content of the hero's consciousness than an independent being.

The action of the novel begins with an erotic triangle that is created by Joaquín himself. In love with his cousin Helena, he brings her together with his friend, as if to assure himself of the other's approval. Helena and Abel, as any novel-reader might have predicted, fall in love.[9] In bringing about the very situation that will torment him for the rest of his life ("I felt in a confused way that I was the one who not only brought them together but made them love each other") Joaquín exposes the duality of his erotic interest; he is as fascinated by Abel as he is by Helena. Abel becomes simultaneously a rival and a model. "That night I was born to the hell of my life."

At first Joaquín describes his passion as hatred, a hatred he decides to hide and nourish in the inmost depths of his soul. Yet he recognizes that all hate is envy – in other words, at once admiration and malice. The envious person longs to be the one he envies, he would like to appropriate his being. Unamuno once said that hate, and especially envy, are forms of love; Joaquín is torn because he feels spite about what he most covets. He wants to be the other and to destroy him. The fundamental unity of his warring impulses reveals itself most tellingly at that moment when he finds himself longing for Abel's hate and envy the way one might long for another's love. " 'If he envied me !' . . . he felt a pleasure that was like melting, a pleasure that made the very marrow of his soul tremble."

If he secretly reveres his enemy, he must hate himself; he hates himself for the reverence and he hates himself for the hatred. Unable to bear the wrath which he has turned against himself, he imagines it as something outside. He dissociates himself from his hatred, describing it as a tumor, a block of ice that has fastened itself to his soul; it is an "invisible enemy", a "guardian demon", a "stinking dragon" with which he grapples. He is not "master of himself, but at once beside himself and possessed". He is not responsible. He keeps thinking that he must have been poisoned; they have given him a hate potion, a "bebedizo", just as Eve gave Cain a philter in her milk. The source of life itself is corrupted and fills the innocent infant with hatefulness and envy.[10] When Joaquín talks about envy as original sin, he is referring both to Adam and Eve's wish to be like God (the idea of original sin is the first displacement, man's first protestation that he is the innocent victim of other's sins) and to the poisoned milk he suckled.

[9] The pattern is similar to Dostoyevsky's *The Eternal Husband*, and the same motif is central to Cervantes's "El Curioso Impertinente".

[10] Melanie Klein writes that "One of the deepest sources of guilt is always linked to envy of the feeding breast, and with the feeling of having spoilt its goodness with envious attacks." *Envy and Gratitude* (London, Tavistock, 1957), p. 29.

Joaquín feels subjugated by his passion. His envy glues him to the rival. He is enraged by Abel's aloofness, yet drawn to it; the other's disdain constitutes his overwhelming allure (just as Helena's coldness arouses his desire). Although he scorns Abel because he is "so full of himself" that he cannot see his own deficiencies, he also would like to appropriate his complacent plenitude (not surprisingly, Abel describes Joaquín in exactly the same terms). That Helena and Abel do not even think of him proves their self-sufficiency; *they* seem totally free, and Joaquín yearns spitefully for that marvelous indifference. The more intensely he feels his dependence, the more desperately he wishes to emulate Abel's apparent freedom, and that wish, of course, binds him ever more securely to the rival.

Joaquín cannot admit to himself that he wants somehow to become Abel, though at one point he comes close to it. When another man confesses his own envy ("if only I could be you!") he says he cannot understand why anyone would want to be someone else. "Being the other is ceasing to be oneself, ceasing to be the self that one is", and that means "ceasing to exist". Unamuno, we remember, often said the same thing. Joaquín asks himself, "and I, who do I want to be?" Since envy is the simultaneous wish to be and not to be, to be the other and to destroy the other (we can compare it to the desire to be everything without ceasing to be oneself), it corrodes the subject's sense of personal substantiality. Hatred of self and hatred of the other go hand in hand, so that the original sense of deprivation and perversity is heightened. Joaquín's is a circular and self-exacerbating passion. The more he envies, the more he hates himself; the more he hates himself, the more he envies.

In one way the wish to absorb the other comes true. Joaquín makes an imagined Abel his constant companion, installing him in the very center of his being. "Even when he was by himself he was never really able to be alone because the other was always there. The other! He even found himself talking to him, imagining what the other said to him." The novel's title is the name of Joaquín's lord and master, his secret self (when Abel is sick, he dares not let him die because his own life depends on that of his enemy). The boundaries of the self are broken and it becomes almost impossible to distinguish the other that is outside from the other that is inside, fantasied rival from real antagonist, Cain from Abel.[11] So Joaquín wonders if perhaps he is envying himself. "I do not love my neighbor, I cannot love him because I do not love myself . . . I cannot love myself." Yet since love and hate are inextricably fused, his rage against himself and against Abel mask a terrible longing – for Abel and for his own self as well. Both self and other seem forever beyond reach yet forever the object of desire and persecution. Towards the end of his life, Joaquín says that Abel has "pursued" him all his life.

Throughout the novel the theme of envy is entwined with the obsession with fame because the two passions are, as Unamuno often pointed out, inseparable (in *Del sentimiento*, Herostratism and envy are used almost synonymously). At a certain point, Joaquín begins to see his passion as a marvelous and grandiose deformity that will guarantee his future renown. His envy turns into arrogance

---

[11] See Paul Ilie's development of this point in "Unamuno, Gorky, and the Cain Myth: Toward a Theory of Personality", *Hispanic Review*, 29 (1961), pp. 310-23.

as he dreams of vindicating himself through the enormity of his evil. He keeps a diary that, though addressed to his daughter, is calculated to amaze future readers. Echoing a passage in Unamuno's own 1897 Diary, Joaquín writes that "we make a spectacle of our most secret and disgusting diseases . . . this very Confession, isn't it something more than an unburdening?" And, just in case the Diary should miss its mark, he also plans another work, a novel which would assure him a place in the "pantheon of the immortal geniuses of his race" and in which he would revenge himself on "the vile world in which he had been forced to live".

It is clear throughout that Joaquín does not covet any of Abel's qualities, for he continually disparages him and insists on his mediocrity, his lack of talent, his cold and unloving personality. What he envies is (after Helena) Abel's renown, his image in the eyes of others; Abel's growing reputation as a painter was a "devastating hail storm in his soul". Since the self that is made in the opinion of others can never be directly experienced, Joaquín chases after a ghost. Not surprisingly, he feels that hallucinatory sense of unreality that Unamuno described so frequently in his essays, and on his death-bed he says that his whole life has been a dream, a painful nightmare. The more he broods on the phantom of the other's glory, the more phantasmal he becomes.

In *Cómo se hace una novela*, Unamuno sees the self which is the product of fame as a double upon which his life depends. Joaquín too is aware that he needs Abel in order to live. We have seen that the "other" who lives within him is alternately or simultaneously his own self or Abel's. Joaquín's envy becomes also an image of self-envy. A year later Unamuno wrote a short story ("Artemio Heutontimoroumenos") whose protagonist is a man divided against himself; Joaquín is such a character. When he attempts to strangle Abel, who then dies of a heart attack, he has, in a sense, murdered a part of himself – his internalized double. He dies a year later.

The doubling motif appears in several other guises as well. The children and the grandchildren (with crossed and duplicated names) repeat and perpetuate the initial pattern of union and rivalry. Abel's painting of Cain and Abel serves as a graphic allusion to the plot. Joaquín's diary and projected novel are also fictionalized reproductions of life; Joaquín says the novel would be a "mirror" of the darkest side of life, a descent into "the depths of human vileness" in which he would, without speaking of himself, put his own soul, expose his own degradation.[12] Yet it would also allow him to appropriate completely the being of his rival ("you will not be Abel Sánchez, but the name I give you. . . . You will live as long as my work lives and your name will drag along the ground behind mine, in the mud"). The novel is at once a mirror, a theft, and a means of perpetuation. In *Niebla, Cómo se hace una novela*, and "Don Sandalio", Unamuno explored those different funtions in terms of literary theory. What is here a minor detail of plot, constitutes in those works the organizing principle of theme and structure.

*   *   *

[12] Unamuno said of *his* novel that he wrote of the plague "not as a doctor but as a sick person". Gullón, *Autobiografías,* p. 119.

In "Artemio Heutontimoroumenos" (1918), more a fictional essay than a short story, the protagonist's two contrary selves never do break apart; the work is not really a double story but a description of the divided consciousness of a self-tormentor. Dealing with the relation between envy and internal splitting, it is a link between *Abel Sánchez* and *El Otro*.

Artemio, "like all men", Unamuno says, has within him two selves, perhaps more, clustered around the two dominant ones that control his thoughts and actions. He compares him to Dr. Jekyll and Mr. Hyde, a man divided into angel and beast. One self, the external and public one, is cynical, efficient and totally lacking in scruples. The internal or private self, which Artemio calls his conscience, is "hypocritical and full of moral concerns". The two antagonists battle constantly but since neither one ever succeeds in overcoming the other, Artemio hates and despises himself. The angelic self hates the demonic one and thus becomes itself demonic; and the public, unscrupulous self despises the other. According to Unamuno this self-hatred and scorn are in large part envy. Each half of the divided personality envies the other; the moral self envies the wholeness and integrity of its opponent. Since envy always conceals a shame-faced admiration, the hidden self admires the efficient and immoral one, but secretly "because he wanted to hide it from himself". Each half must want at once to supplant the other and to destroy it. Both fail. Disconsolate about the frustration of his worldly ambitions, Artemio rankles under his own austerity and apparent virtue. Envious of himself, he torments and devours himself. The two selves finally fuse into a single one in which the angelic is lost in the demonic; he finds himself too cowardly to do good and too cowardly to do evil.

The struggle, Unamuno says, is between ambition and pride, and although he does not define those terms here, we know that the first (the aim of the external self) has to do with fame and that the second (the aim of the internal self) refers to self-possession. Unamuno knew this kind of division at first hand and he once described himself as heutontimoroumenos,[13] attributing the splitting and self-destructive frenzy to his loss of faith in immortality and the consequent intensification of the need for fame. Since both "ambition" and "pride" pursue an impossibly concrete and stable identity, they divide and ultimately destroy the subject. The struggle between Artemio's inner and outer selves ends in "the destruction of both, each by the other".

* * *

The play *El Otro* (*The Other*, 1926, XII, 800-62) reduces the complex of ambition, fame-seeking, envy, and internal splitting to the last two terms and presents a formula statement of their relation. It is one of Unamuno's most explicit descriptions of internal division. Only here it is presented as real – Cosme and Damián are twin brothers. Unamuno uses the names of the famous pair of friends in hagiography for two inseparable enemies. One has killed the other but we do not know which. The survivor is called "el Otro," and he lives in Cosme's house with Cosme's wife, Laura, who had once been courted by both brothers.

[13] *Epistolario a Clarín*, p. 86.

"El Otro" refuses to divulge his identity. In telling a friend about the murder, he describes a scene very similar to the one in "El que se enterró" – a doubling and a death. "I saw myself as if I had peeled myself off a mirror." He felt his consciousness dissolving. "I began to live or unlive backwards in time . . . my life unrolled before me and I was once again twenty years old, then ten, then five . . . and when I felt on my infant's lips the taste of holy mother's milk – I was unborn – I died." On regaining consciousness he was seated in the place of the other, facing his own corpse. "I am the dead one. . . . Everything is a mirror for me." The mirror disintegrates the sense of individuality so that the return to the double birth signals the death of one of the twins. In this account, the character's "memory" of the initial doubling stands in place of the death of his twin; the past blocks out the present in a way that both conceals and reveals the tie between division and destruction.

"El Otro" gives Damiana a different version of the event : two twins who, like Jacob and Esau, had fought in their mother's womb, fall in love with the same woman; "full of hate for themselves and bent on mutual suicide" they fight; one kills the other. We cannot even be sure which woman they were disputing, Laura or Damiana. The two women, in love with both twins, compete for the possession of the survivor, each one claiming that the "Other" killed for her sake. "El Otro", like Juan in *Dos Madres*, finds himself torn between two furies. "Between the two of you, you are killing me." He shoots himself and is buried with his brother.

If in *Abel Sánchez*, envy and hate led to a confusion between self and enemy, here an original biological doubling causes envy and hate. The causal sequence seems to be reversed. "El Otro" hates himself because he sees himself outside of himself; he speaks of a terrible rivalry and of the shame of being distinguished only by a name. He hates his brother and claims it was he who taught him to hate himself. It becomes clear as the play develops, however, that Unamuno is using twinship as a concrete representation of a psychological state, a dramatic embodiment of Joaquín's assertion that envy is a form of kinship. Twinship is presented as both the cause and the symbol of internal splitting and envious self-hate. The twin is a double (there is, of course, a long association of the two themes in the history of man's thought). This confusion of biological fact and metaphorical usage allows Unamuno to present doubling as an unexplained and inexplicable phenomenon. And thanks to this confusion he can dramatize the ever-intensifying dynamics of envy, malice, and splitting while at the same time concealing the nature of their true relationship. Yet those connections are evident in the dialogue and in the whole structure of the plot.

"El Otro" hates his mirror image. It is as if visibility made one vulnerable. Whatever he hopes to find within himself is always belied by the visible self – the other. And that separation is deadly. "To see oneself is to die – or to kill oneself." He hates himself for being no different from the other, his twin – for being no different from others in general. The twin tie is an emblem of a lack of distinction that is made all the more acute by the murder, for after his brother's death he loses even the distinction of his name, disappearing completely behind an alienated and alienating designation. In this play "the other" is a linguistic shifter that cannot be defined by its context; on the contrary, the context is what makes it undefineable; it shifts back and forth between two indistinguishable passions.

The processes Unamuno describes in *El Otro* can have no resolution. They intensify and repeat themselves. The structure of the play and the disposition of its characters sharpen the image of an infernal circularity broken only by death. The two women are like looking-glass reflections of the two brothers; Laura calls Damiana "Caina" and she calls her "Abela". Each character plays reversible roles in the drama of master and slave, possessor and possessed; Damiana says "you have possessed me . . . No, I have possessed you", and "el Otro" claims that the seducer is really the seduced. Damiana and Laura are indistinguishable for him and for the reader as well. The terrible rivalry and envy between like persons, this duel to the death for illusory distinctions, is projected into the future so that the next generation will mirror this one. Damiana is expecting a child – of either Cosme or Damián – perhaps twins because she feels them struggling in her womb. If *Dos madres, La tía Tula* and *Abel Sánchez* show the increasing isolation and dependence of the person who attempts to achieve his being through the other and against others, *El Otro* shows the last and most frenzied stage of the pursuit of the self in which extreme isolation and extreme dependence combine in an assault on the other that is also the annihilation of the self.

Yet the play's epilogue suggests another way out. The housekeeper, who has refused to identify "el Otro", insists on the need to preserve the mystery, indeed, to preserve all mystery. "Mystery is fatefulness – Destiny – let us close our eyes to mystery. The uncertainty of our final hour permits us to live, the secret of our destiny, of our true personality, lets us dream – Let us dream then, without looking for a solution to the dream. Life is a dream." She shifts from the specific theme of the play to a broader and less defineable one – the secret of personality – so that the drama of self-division and internalized spite can be re-cast as the general problem of all humanity. In like manner, Unamuno, in a prologue written in 1932, said that the play had sprung from his "obsession" with the "mystery of personality" and the "anguished sentiment of our identity and individual continuity" (XII, 801), indicating that the "Other's" drama is indeed everyman's. The housekeeper's plea then might mean that the only alternative to murder and suicide is what Unamuno once called the "hypnotic sense of life" – the dream. The "mystery of personality", a formula which is already a blurring of the concrete processes depicted in the play, thus passes over to a broad metaphysical mystification.[14]

---

[14] Unamuno's mystifications lead some critics to interpret his stories of self-division as demonstrations of the malleability and multiplicity of personality; for example, Gullón: "The image of the split expresses the fluidity of being, the incessant undulation in which the soul molds and transforms itself" (op. cit., p. 171).

III

From Novel to Dream

"La novela de don Sandalio, jugador de ajedrez" ("Don Sandalio, Chess Player", 1930, XVI, 629-70) is a curious novella; purporting to tell no story at all, it hovers ambiguously between fiction and confession. The narrator presents two persons – himself and Don Sandalio – who could become characters in a novel but who appear instead as the supports of a self-conscious disquisition on the fictitiousness of personality and the reality of fiction. Since the narrator is a duplicate of the author, the work takes the form of a story within a story, recalling the technique and theme of *Cómo se hace una novela*.

The narrative is presented as a collection of letters sent to Unamuno by an unknown correspondent and addressed to a man named Felipe. The letter-writer tells about his stay in a small coastal town where he has gone to get away from it all; he is suffering from "anthrophobia". His only "friends", he says, are an old hollow oak tree covered by the green leaves of a vine, and the ruins of a farmhouse with a burned-out hearth covered with ivy. Both are images of symbolic importance, suggesting isolation and death but also their opposites, reconciliation, complementarity, and renewal. The only human being in this solitary existence is a certain Don Sandalio who plays chess all day in the casino; the narrator watches him fascinated and begins to spin a web of fantasy about the taciturn and self-absorbed man. One day the two play chess together and from then on meet for daily games, though they never speak to each other. Little by little the writer supplants the real Don Sandalio with an imaginary one whom he calls "my Don Sandalio". He distinguishes between the man who plays chess in the casino and "the other one, the one who has gone into the depths of my soul and follows me everywhere. I dream of him. I almost suffer with him".

The obsessive dream is never described; the imaginary Don Sandalio remains for the reader an unknown creature hidden in the mind of the dreamer. But at the point where the writer wonders if Don Sandalio has replaced his own self, if he is "suffering from a dual personality", we must conclude that the compelling figure is a mirror image, the projection of his own solitude and incommunicability. The imaginary Don Sandalio is a double. No wonder he finds that "this Don Sandalio is driving me mad".

Since the doubled person is a divided one, the narrator longs to repossess himself; he would like to get from his mirrored self his own reflection. He asks himself, "What does he think of me? What am I like for him? Who am I for him?" But one's image in the mind of a phantom must be phantasmal. The dual symbolic implications of vine-covered oak and vine-covered ruins give way to

the single meaning of emptiness; the hollow tree and burned-out hearth duplicate the writer's own inner being.

The narrator is determined not to know anything about the flesh-and-blood
chess partner; when people offer him bits of information, he resolutely rejects
them. But one day the outer world threatens to intrude upon the charmed circle
of the *solus ipse*. Don Sandalio does not appear at the casino and someone says
that his son has died. A few days later the writer hears the surprising news that
Don Sandalio has been put in jail. He does not want to find out why because
he wants to keep his Don Sandalio "pure and uncontaminated". "I don't want
any stories [*historias*]. Stories? When I need them, I'll invent them." As Unamuno said in *Cómo se hace una novela*, all true "histories" are novels. Invention
replaces fact, and fiction spins out of a void in the heart of "reality".

When he learns that Don Sandalio has died in jail, he is grief stricken; a
dazed "somnambulist", he goes off to the woods and curls up in the hollow of
the old oak and "begins to dream" (no sooner does one dream end than another
begins). He feels within him an immense emptiness (a hollow within a hollow).
He wonders if the other invented him too and if he is perhaps only the projection of the other's fantasy. He recalls an empty provincial café where he once
saw himself multiply reflected in the fogged mirrors lining the walls; that "sad
illusion" had made him think of a monastery of solitary men, all copies of one
original.

As time passes he comes to accept his partner's death but he begins to feel
haunted by the ghost of the "real" Don Sandalio, the one with the son, the one
who died in jail. One night he thinks he sees this ghost on the street, running
away from him so as not to be recognized. There is a split here between the
fantasied Don Sandalio who has been incorporated and identified with the
writer's own self, and the "real one" outside; we might compare the external
Don Sandalio to the external self. Thus, the real-life Don Sandalio is an emblem of self-estrangement.[1]

In this world of confused boundaries, the narrator comes to doubt his own
memories. "No one can be sure of what has happened and what he continually
imagines has happened." Fantasy and reality merge in a disturbing fashion.
But rather than admit uneasiness, the letter-writer argues that the confusion of
fiction and reality is central to human existence. Like Unamuno, this narrator
has a fondness for uncertainty (in *Del sentimiento trágico* he speaks of "consoling
uncertainty") and the mystery of dim mirrors. He wilfully proclaims the deceptiveness of everything. The maneuver, however, does not work because he begins
to fear his own inventiveness and the ease with which he falls into fantasy. "And
now I am afraid that on the death of Don Sandalio I am creating another Don
Sandalio. But I am afraid? Fear? Why?" He does not answer – doubtless cannot
answer – this question. Although he is eager to invent imaginary people, he is
also terrified by the possibility of success. He talks constantly about "his" Don

---

[1] In Hawthorn's "Monsieur de Miroir", the author wonders if the title character (whom
he had "loved well") will haunt him after death "to remind the neglected world of one
who has staked so much to win a name". See Rogers (*The Double in Literature*, p. 21),
who also points out that pursuer and pursued are frequent double figures (p. 62).

Sandalio, yet now expresses amazement and fear at the apparent autonomy of that creation. "The novel of Don Sandalio" seems to impose itself upon him. Like the sorcerer's apprentice, he is frightened by his own fantasmagoria.

This simultaneous attraction and fear of fantasy determine the emotional tenor of the story and constitute its central theme, though it is rather indirectly presented through the writer's theories on the craft of fiction. Thus he argues that he is not interested in facts and documentation; if Felipe wants more of a story, he should write or dream it up himself. After all, being a novelist is much better than being a consumer of the fictions of others. "If it is terrible to fall into the profession of fabricator of novels, it is even more terrible to fall into the profession of novel-reader." He scorns the reader who, permitting himself no liberties with "reality", vicariously enjoys the inventions of others. Obviously, fiction-making involves a peculiar anxiety.

In the epilogue Unamuno tells us that in re-reading the letters he was overcome by the suspicion that the whole thing is a fiction devised to present a "kind of clever autobiography".[2] Don Sandalio, he suggests, is himself the author of the letters; he wants to represent himself and at the same time hide the truth of that representation. Maybe Don Sandalio is "dear Felipe" – a single character in a hall of mirrors. This fusion suggests to Unamuno another one, that of human novelist and divine one; like God (in his "Divine Novel"), the novelist creates himself in his work. Novelist and God merge in the generative act. This exalted dream replaces the actual task of writing an ordinary human novel. Unamuno here prefers theory to practice; his goal is "the novel of the novel – something like the shadow of a shadow". His readers can supply their own plots. Unamuno says "my readers do not look for the coherent world of so-called realistic novels – my readers know that a plot is nothing but the pretext for a novel and that the novel remains more whole and more pure . . . more novelistic, if you remove the plot". In the epilogue Unamuno strives for an identification both with God and with his readers. That attempted merging counterbalances what occurred in the novel – an imaginary incorporation that was also an internal splitting. Self-estrangement, as always, calls up the desire for fusion.

We might ask why Unamuno and the letter writer are being so mysterious, so reticent, so anxious. As I said, we are told about the narrator's fantasy of Don Sandalio but we are never let in on the fantasy itself. Why? In one of his last letters, the narrator brings up the issue of the characters intentionally excluded from his account – that is the women who must have figured in Don Sandalio's life. "I know you, Felipe . . . in all my letters you have missed the figure of a woman and now you imagine that the novel you are looking for . . . will begin to take shape as soon as she appears . . . 'cherchez la femme'. But I do not intend to look for Don Sandalio's daughter or for any other female with whom he might have some connection. I think that for Don Sandalio there was no woman but the chess queen . . . that queen who dominates the chess board,

[2] At a certain point in his life (during his University days in Madrid), Unamuno considered his own addiction to chess an almost unconquerable vice; he too played with a little old man whose identity he never knew. See Rudd, op. cit., p. 57.

but whose imperial dignity can be attained, through a sex change, by a lowly pawn. This I believe was the only queen of his thoughts."

Since Don Sandalio is the narrator's projected reflection, we must assume that the only woman in his life too is the chess queen. Just as a novel writer identifies himself with the Divine Author, the lowly pawn might become a queen. The narrator draws from his mind his own beloved image and inserts it in the body of another; it is a kind of male parthenogenesis. Both God and the chess queen are images of a totally autonomous and free creativity. Since what is created is an alter-ego, the novelist, as Unamuno so often said, creates himself. In one way the story is a half-veiled fantasy about giving birth – queen-like – to a creature one has engendered upon oneself. The narrator becomes the father of himself – or, more accurately, his mother – both mother and child. But since the dream of self-creation also means division and destruction, the dreamer turns away from his alarming vision. The whole matter is so unsettling that the story never really gets told and we are left with a commentary about the act of fantasy in which the author sets himself at a distance from his subject.

The novel is replete with distancing devices. The author puts on several narrative masks – he is the "Unamuno" who addresses the reader directly, he is the first person narrator, he is Don Sandalio, he is Felipe. It is worth noting that Unamuno's fictions rarely have narrators who are themselves characters. Most are told by the omniscient author. The narrator-witness or narrator-protagonist invariably appears, however, in his stories of the double. "El que se enterró" is told by a friend of the protagonist; "Artemio" by an acquaintance. In *El otro* and *Abel Sánchez*, parts of the work are the protagonists' versions. When Joaquín's envy is at fever pitch, the omniscient narrator cedes his place to Joaquín's diary. The character splits himself in two and the author doubles himself in his narrator. Theme and structure are strictly coordinated.

Besides the central omission of plot or character there are other omissions in the novella, the most significant being the theme of envy, which is nowhere mentioned but which is evident in certain characteristic associations. In the beginning the narrator compares himself to Robinson Crusoe (a figure who greatly interested Unamuno);[3] in an essay written the same year, "La ciudad de Henoch" ("The City of Enoch"), he says that Robinson was fleeing from the envious passions that rule society. In "Don Sandalio", the narrator compares the café to a monastery of solitary men; in the essay Unamuno describes monasteries as incubators of envy. *Abel Sánchez* and *El otro* explicitly portray the link between envy and doubling. "Don Sandalio" elaborates the theme in its very absence.

Absence is the core of the novel. The images of the hollow oak and the aban-

---

[3] In *Serious Reflections of Robinson Crusoe with His Vision of the Angelic World* (London, 1790), chapter I "Of Solitude", Defoe has Robinson view the "stage of life which we act upon in this world" and decide that "life in general is, or ought to be, but one universal act of solitude . . . The world, I say, is nothing to us . . . all reflection is carried home, and our dear self is, in one respect, the end of living. Hence man may be properly said to be *alone* in the midst of the crowds and hurry of men of business." Like Unamuno, Crusoe looks for "true solitude" in the middle of the crowded city. Missing from Robinson's idealization of solitude (and from Unamuno's comments on it) is the exploitation and servitude of Friday.

doned hearth duplicate the inner emptiness of the narrator and the mystery of Don Sandalio's personality (in the prologue Unamuno says the inner being of Don Sandalio escapes us – "or perhaps he has none"). Around these empty spaces he weaves a narrative web about an obsessive longing for another who turns out to be the self. Heightened and inflamed by its sheer impossibility, this reflexive desire simultaneously allures and repels. The narrator's fear is the fear of his own self-consuming passion.

If the content that is evaded is self-desire, what stands in its place is what the author sees as the disturbing and fundamental unity of the creative act (making a fiction) and the act of annihilation (dissolving the concrete world of reality into fiction). The situation seems to be : he fantasies the other and the other fantasies him, therefore neither of them exists. Fiction and reality merge and an all-pervasive doubt becomes the only reality. To counter the doubt he identifies himself as novelist with the creator of all reality, with God. The writer's ability to make or dissolve the world confers simultaneously – or alternately – a heady sense of power and an uneasy sense of shame or guilt against which he defends himself by protesting that, after all, it is better to write novels than to read them. An intense ambivalence about making fictions, about telling stories, leads him to multiply narrative disguises. He covers his tracks and resorts to the standard Unamunian technique of drawing the reader into the creative act – you, dear reader, make the story and supply the plot.

In "Don Sandalio" we move then from the theme of the double as a psychological phenomenon to the problematical relation between the author and his work. Fiction-making has become almost a forbidden game. This is a recurrent theme in modern literature and certain contemporary writers – one thinks of Borges or Nabokov (also intrigued with mirrors and doubles) – elaborate it with dazzling artfulness. Unamuno's works do not approach the highly self-conscious irony of those writers. For him the subject can still be dealt with on the level of philosophical speculation. In this story, as well as in *Niebla* and *Cómo se hace una novela*, he tends to resolve the tension between "fiction" and "reality" in favor of the first.

The novelists's final gambit is, of course, the identification of private dream and objective creation. He seeks to make the hollow itself into substance, thereby showing that the empty womb, the "masculine" mind, can bring forth life. "La novela de don Sandalio" is a metaphorical fulfillment of the dream of "Plenitud de plenitudes" – absence is fullness.

*   *   *

Niebla (*Mist*, 1914, II, 783-1000) has received more critical attention than any of Unamuno's other novels. It is a puzzling mixture of stylistic tones, of fictional invention and philosophical argument. Critics have regarded it as a statement about Unamuno's own metaphysical concerns, and the author himself obviously did too. Since Unamuno often said that a novelist makes himself in his work and since in *Niebla* he chooses to appear before his readers as both author and character, some people speak of a self-creative process. The protagonist, Augusto Pérez, who constantly talks about how he has been awakened to real life through love and suffering, is also said to create himself, to emerge from the "mist" into true consciousness. The parallel efforts of novelist and character are taken as evidence of Unamuno's success in merging fiction and reality, as if the aspirations of the character, shared by his author, could actually come true.[4]

Unamuno handles his narrative material in two different ways. Although there is no formal separation, we could divide the novel into two parts; most of it is devoted to the somewhat humorous story of Augusto Pérez, but the last three chapters (beginning in Chapter XXX when the hero first thinks of suicide and including the famous scene between him and his author) shift to a serious examination of the character's problems that sounds very much like one of Unamuno's essays.[5] Thus, while much of the work follows the classic novelistic formula of delusion and its ironic exposure (so well described by Ortega in *Meditaciones del Quijote*), the final chapters modify that perspective by suggesting a collusive agreement in values between character and author. Of course, the reader cannot help but be aware that both have many ideas in common; Augusto, the bumbler, the *panoli*, often says just what Unamuno says in his essays. But if the first part of the book casts those ideas within the ironic framework of the character's foolish plight, the second part argues quite seriously for their philosophical correctness. *Niebla* oscillates between comedy and dead-serious exhortation.

The novel's popularity is probably due to the readers' interest in the philosophical theme itself, in the author's circular and apparently endless speculations on the problematical relation between what is real and what is made-up. It is this continually shifting focus between the hazards and the rewards of fiction that creates the structural and conceptual imbalance. The novel teeters back and forth, and the author clearly finds it difficult to come to any kind of conclusion. His reluctance to bring his book to a close is evident in his own intervention (which projects the work into the reader's own life), in the paradoxical twists and reversals of the epilogue, in the prologue supposedly written by one of the characters (Víctor Goti), in the "post-prologue", and in the "Historia de *Niebla*" that Unamuno wrote some twenty-one years later. An ending represents resolution – but also death. In 1904 ("A lo que salga") Unamuno wrote that "only in novelistic fictions do things have a definite beginning and a definite ending. May this essay never end! May none of my works ever end! My God, may my life never end!" Against ending, against death, Unamuno sets a non-novelistic fiction (a *nivola*) through which he hopes to elude certain hard facts of "reality".

"A lo que salga", we remember, also describes his vision of a "future reign of the spirit" when men's souls would congeal in a common spiritual mist, a single soul in which would float the outer shells that now separate us from each

---

[4] See, among others, Ricardo Gullón, "El Amigo Manso, entre Galdós y Unamuno", *Mundo Nuevo*, no. 4 (Oct., 1966); Geoffrey Ribbans, "The Structure of Unamuno's *Niebla*", *Spanish Thought and Letters in the Twentieth Century*; Leon Livingstone, "The Novel as Self-Creation", in *Unamuno Creator and Creation*; Ruth House Webber, "Kierkegaard and the Elaboration of Unamuno's *Niebla*", *Hispanic Review*, 32 (1964); Ciriaco Morón-Arroyo, "*Niebla* en la evolución temática de Unamuno", *MLN*, 81, No. 2 (1966), 143-58.

[5] A. A. Parker summarizes the different critical reactions to the novel's split in "On the Interpretation of *Niebla*", in *Unamuno, Creator and Creation*, pp. 116-38.

other. Returning to that vision ten years later Unamuno cannot decide if the mist means a common salvation or an individual annihilation. He chooses both possibilities at once, entangling them so thoroughly in his narrative that the reader cannot separate the author's dreams or wishes – the private fiction – from the public fiction which is the novel. *Niebla*'s ambiguity is not so much the result of a consciously controlled representation of the impenetrability of reality (the standard interpretation) as a reflection of the author's own internal contradictions.

The story opens with the appearance of Augusto in the doorway of his house. From the beginning the narrator situates us within the observing consciousness of his protagonist, a consciousness given to interminable and uninterrupted speculation. Thus we come to know both the character and his surroundings through a rambling train of thoughts, presented sometimes in indirect interior monologues, sometimes through soliloquies that incorporate what is seen and heard. The outside world of city streets, automobiles, passers-by is woven into the fabric of an internal meditation that continually posits an ideal of self-sufficiency, passivity, and pure contemplation ("the noblest function of things is to be contemplated"). Augusto's imagination, as he tells himself, never rests. He is a tireless commentator and he has a theory about everything. But he is willing to take certain cues from external events; indeed, he lets them suggest to him the course of his lively inner discourse. Thus, waiting for some sign to show which way he should walk, his eyes are caught by a lovely young woman whom he follows "as if magnetized" to the entrance of her house. He does what is customary in such a situation – asks the concierge for information and begins to play the role of admirer. From then on, "sweet Eugenia" fills his thoughts, becoming his most private creation. Like the narrator in "Don Sandalio", he insists on his rights of authorship. "My Eugenia, yes mine . . . the one that I am forging alone, not the other one, not the one of flesh and blood." Unamuno creates a character whose novelistic life begins with the creation of another character. The love story told in *Niebla* explores the consequences of this internal duplication.

Augusto's infatuation has very little to do with the flesh and blood woman. Immersed in day-dreams, he repeatedly passes her in the street without seeing her because, as the narrator says, "the spiritual mist was too dense". In love with his own emotions, he plans to court the woman he himself has invented. Although he wonders at one point how he can be in love with someone he does not even know, he assures himself that *conocimiento* ("acquaintance" or "knowledge"; Unamuno plays on both meanings of the word) will come later. Knowledge, however, can be threatening : "Love precedes knowledge (*conocimiento*) and knowledge kills it." From the first he worries about the intrusion of reality into the private dream. Love is a "glimmer in the mist", that is ever in danger of condensing into the rain or hail of "science". Since "knowledge" and "science" destroy love, Augusto prefers indefinition and vagueness – "mist, mist !" Throughout the novel he struggles to protect the dream from various kinds of unwelcome knowledge.

The narrative connects the protagonist's distraction with the death of his mother some six months earlier. For many years he had lived alone with her (his father, a "mythical shadow", died when he was very young) and now, cut loose and adrift, he feels like a sleepwalker in the "mist" of everyday reality. He lived as a "part" of his mother, "in a sweet dream". So love for him is a mutually absorbing dream in which one loses any sense of independent identity. "Oh, Eugenia . . . dream of me and with me!" The title image, which has many different connotations,[6] embodies the character's contradictory yearnings; he longs to lose himself in the mist of love yet he feels anxious about his somnambulistic estrangement and hopes that love will give him a sense of substance and reality. Dazedly he moves through the prescribed stages of courtship while Unamuno's comic contriving gently mocks his romantic pretentions.

His many philosophical disquisitions on love (addressed to his dog Orfeo) reproduce some of the patterns of Unamuno's essays. In both cases the paradoxical idea of solipsistic communion (the shared dream) causes a break with the objective, observable self. He wonders if Eugenia is a creation of his or he of her, or if they are both mutual creations and the world a circular chain of dreamers. Augusto experiences the same hallucinatory dissociation that Unamuno described in some essays; he sometimes thinks that he is not there and that others cannot see him, or he imagines they do not see him as he sees himself and that when he thinks he is behaving in a perfectly ordinary way, he is really playing the fool and everyone is laughing at him. Only love can give him a sense of solid self; "thanks to love I feel the bulk of my soul. I touch it. My soul begins to pain me in its very center" (pain, we remember from *Del sentimiento trágico*, returns consciousness to itself).

Augusto also, we have seen, links knowledge and love. When Eugenia's uncle talks about knowledge in the Biblical sense of the word, he thinks of the common confusion between sexuality and the fall of Adam and Eve for having tasted the fruit of the tree of knowledge of good and evil. These interchangeable forms of "knowledge" shed light on his rejection of science for the comforting blur of the mist and give a new significance to his statement that "love precedes knowledge and knowledge kills it". He even finds rationality "sinful". In order to avoid "knowledge" he retreats to a fantasy world of pure spirituality; when he finds he has a rival he tells himself that the other may possess her physically but that the "spiritual light" in her eyes is his alone. As his friend Víctor points out, his love is cerebral; he himself might be merely an idea, a "fictitious entity". Augusto's sentiments are derived from novels ("things you read in books", as Eugenia says) because fiction is a refuge from the real world. Yet this deter-

---

[6] Mist first refers to the details of everyday life. But it is also opposed to knowledge and science as consoling confusion and refuge from reality. In this sense, it is synonymous with dream, and dream is always tied to Augusto's unconscious existence when he "formed a part" of his mother. Dream often represents the ideal of merging or non-separation ("what is the real world but the dream we all dream, the common dream?"). But both mist and dream have a contrary affective charge too. Augusto is trying to get out of the mist; he hopes love will dissipate or congeal it. When he does not succeed in love, he sees himself as a somnambulist; "for years I have wandered like a ghost, like a puppet of mist, without believing in my own existence." Yet one of the remedies Víctor proposes for his ontological malady is the intentional confounding of dream and wakefulness.

minedly fictitious person keeps telling himself (and convincing the novel's commentators) that Eugenia has awakened him to real life.

As the character eagerly proclaims his new-found sense of self, the author points up his dreamy mystifications. He falls in love with the laundry girl, Rosario, without even realizing it. Consistently he conceals from himself the meaning of his own acts and feelings, elaborating this denial of reality in an intellectual justification of fantasy. Language, Augusto says, is a screen between reality and consciousness; whenever man speaks, he lies. Words, gestures, and all other forms of conventional expression generate sensations and feelings that would otherwise not exist. Thus the world comes into being thanks to fabulation. But that means, for Augusto, that all human culture is an empty theatrical show. "We are all personae, masks, actors. No one suffers or enjoys what he says he suffers and enjoys . . . At bottom, we are quite unmoved." By seeing himself as both actor and spectator, Augusto disowns his own words and deeds; like Robleda, he seeks to hide behind the role and thus shield himself from others' eyes.

The consequence of this defensive strategy is that "at bottom we are quite unmoved". The price paid for evasion is that we constantly suspect we are unreal. The performer needs the collaboration of an audience in order to confirm his existence; being a spectator to himself does not really do the trick. And Augusto's plight is that the others either use him or ignore him; Eugenia and his rival Mauricio treat him as "a puppet, an object, a nobody" – and "I have my character, I certainly do. I am I". This affirmation of self is, however, undermined by the indifference of others. In the street, in the midst of hurrying crowds that pay no attention to him, "that I of 'I am I' grew smaller and smaller until it retreated inside his body and looked there for some corner in which to curl up so no one would see it". He becomes "a shadow, a phantom . . . he did not feel himself". Augusto depends on others for his very being. So does his friend Víctor who, when he faces the mirror alone, imagines he is a "dream", a "fictitious entity".

Since real mirrors can play such strange tricks, he seeks proof of his existence in the eyes of another. Augusto asks Rosario if he can look at himself in her eyes because only in that way can he come to know himself (this sounds almost like an unwitting play on the "knowledge" motif, a comic inversion of sexual knowledge). But turning another person into a mirror denies the subjectivity needed to acknowledge one's own.[7] Though Rosario does not submit with docility. "The mirror looked at him in a strange way"; she thinks he must be mad. And when he thinks about it later he too decides that his body must do certain things of which he is unaware; once again he wonders if when he goes down the street "like a normal person" he is really acting the fool and others are mocking him. He wonders if he is crazy. If he is crazy, he is not responsible. He would prefer to have people laugh at a madness he cannot control than at his own absurd

---

[7] "This approach impels me to get hold of the other and to constitute him as an object to discover there my own object-state. But this is to kill the hen that lays the golden eggs." Jean Paul Sartre, *Being and Nothingness*, tr. Hazel Barnes (New York: Philosophical Library, 1956), p. 291.

actions. When he discovers that Rosario and Mauricio have been making fun of him, he is plunged back into the mist.

Augusto seems constantly threatened by invisibility. Yet visibility frightens him because he would like to think that he is not what others see. He needs others (or the image they reflect of him) to confirm his existence, yet others threaten to destroy him. He must have felt that falling in love with an imaginary Eugenia would have protected him from the hazards of existence. But precisely because he was so absorbed in his dream, the real Eugenia was able to use him for her own ends. When Augusto discovers this, the invented world collapses and he receives the news of her elopement with Mauricio with a calm that "made him doubt his own existence".

In their last conversation (Chapter XXX) Augusto's friend Víctor tries to convince him of the benefits of self-doubt; he advises Augusto to joke about himself and to turn against everything with corrosive mockery. "One must corrode and confuse . . . Confuse the dream with wakefulness, fiction with reality, true with false; confuse it all in a single mist." Furthermore, Augusto should devour himself because, explains Víctor, the pain of being devoured will be neutralized by the pleasure of devouring so that he will become "a mere spectacle" for himself. Augusto's error has been thinking that he is a concrete and palpable entity. Víctor comes close to arguing that the self is an illusion from which one must be freed. According to him, the liberating effect of art is that it makes one doubt his own existence. But doubt, as all of Unamuno's works show, is not the same as liberation. It heightens the obsession with the self and the need to defend it against the others. The image of devouring suggests an aggression turned inwards; instead of the mutually inflicted pain and the cannibalism described in Chapter XI of *Del sentimiento trágico*, Víctor proposes a solipsistic mode of destructiveness that is appropriately paired with an assault on the external world. Instead of counseling his friend to disillusion himself about his ego, Víctor suggests the opposite – turning the external world into dream and fantasy. Both agree that the pain of self-immolation brings about a new birth. Augusto imagines that at last he has come into being; he has become "the father of himself".

Yet the fantasy of the self as *causa sui* leads directly to its opposite – the image of the self as a fiction created by someone else. In his interview with "Unamuno" (Chapter XXXI), Augusto learns that he is nothing but the author's invention. He counters that Unamuno is nothing but a pretext for the appearance of Augusto and that the author has no existence beyond that established by his characters. As another character had pointed out earlier, everyone depends on everyone else. "No one is the one he is but the one that others make him." After Augusto's death the doctor says that "a person is the one who knows least about his existence . . . one does not exist except for others". Thus everyone is a projected image, a fictitious entity. And if the whole world is fiction, then fiction must be the only reality. Far from accepting the idea that the self is a mirage or an illusion, Víctor, Augusto, and Unamuno (both as character and as author) turn the evidence around and affirm that the universe itself is imaginary.

Augusto's theory of fantasy denies the reality of feeling and sentiment. Only

words exist. "What is there that is not something out of a book? Before books
... before words, before thought, was there anything?" The epilogue, a monologue by the dog Orfeo, reaffirms the delusiveness of speech; language makes
men hypocrites, actors, and frauds. The world of words supplants the real one,
so that for man everything is unreal and made-up.

The confounding of fiction and reality takes us back to where the whole story
began. Augusto had fallen in love with his own fantasy of Eugenia. The source
of all his troubles was his unwillingness to accept the distinctions between wish
and fact. This was the comic principle that determined the course of events, but
now, since Unamuno, the author, is speaking through Víctor, Augusto, the
"Unamuno" of the interview, and paradoxically, through Orfeo too, comedy is
abandoned for metaphysical speculation. Such shifts occurred earlier for brief
moments throughout the novel. For instance, when Augusto says love is an
ecstasy that takes us out of ourselves, the smile of the concierge "brought him
back to reality – to reality?" So too, some of Augusto's musings on reality and
fiction – "what is the real world but the dream we all dream, the common
dream?" – suspend the comic pattern that ridicules self-delusion. Although the
private dream of Augusto's love is often enough exposed to the mockery of
events, the metaphysical notion of the world as dream appears as a serious motif
in the public fiction of the novel. The humorous contrast between fiction and
reality gives way at times to a philosophical statement about their unity.

The movement from a comic treatment to a serious one appears to be reversed
with Augusto's death, which really looks like one last joke on the poor man's
metaphysical pretensions. After a huge meal of steaks, omelettes, cold-cuts,
cheeses, and fruits, he gets sick and dies. Most critics take this quite seriously,
even asking (along with Víctor) whether it was not a suicide. Blanco Aguinaga
says Augusto has finally "passed from being an Object . . . to being a Subject".
But aside from the character's own assertions, there is no evidence whatsoever
of any "well-earned acquisition of consciousness".[8] For a man as spiritual as
Augusto, over-eating is a pretty funny way to die. The possibility of tragedy only
arises because of the shift from the irony of the plot to the seriousnes of the
arguments in the last chapters.

Throughout the work, Unamuno takes pains to establish distinctions which
are later denied. In the prologue, Víctor Goti explains that Unamuno always
wanted to write a comic tragedy or a tragic farce, fusing and confusing the two.
The fusion parallels that between fiction and reality, character and author. And
certainly Unamuno and Augusto have a lot in common. Both believe that love
should be pain and compassion; both tend to negate the meaning of words and
acts by asserting that everything is play-acting. Both want to live on in the
memories of their readers, "an eternal soul, eternally suffering". Both prefer the
fantasy of the other to his concrete presence (the genesis of Eugenia in Augusto's
mind reproduces the opening paragraph of the essay "Soledad"; in each case,
the other is recreated in consciousness on the basis of the remembered vision of

---

[8] Blanco Aguinaga, "Unamuno's *Niebla*: Existence and the Game of Fiction", *MLN*,
79, No. 2 (1964), p. 204.

the eyes);[9] both find it easier to love the imaginary projection than the real person it displaces ("that is why I flee from him in order to seek him and avoid him because I love him"). When Augusto and Unamuno share so many attitudes how can we keep philosophy and comedy apart? Or fiction and reality?

The leveling of barriers between the real world and the fictitious one is invariably a vehicle for a commentary on the artist's craft. It is also a kind of philosophical image that can have several different meanings. The world as theater or novel may refer to the brevity of life, the vanity of earthly glory, and man's subordination to God. Although Unamuno developed some aspects of this traditional symbol in certain early essays (for example, "La vida es sueño"), he did not use it in his fictional works. The metaphor may also serve as a reminder of the limits of human knowledge, indicating either the multiplicity of error or the multiplicity of truth; categories like "real" and "fictitious" can be playfully subverted in order to demonstrate the deceptiveness of all ideas. But such relativizing irony is foreign to Unamuno's anxious concern with identity and perpetuation. For Unamuno the device suggests alternate modes of existence; intrigued with the relation between the literary character and the real person, he sometimes argued that the former might be more real and more intense than the person who lives "in the ordinary way" ("Sobre le lectura del Quijote" [1905] III, 842-60). Such a view illuminates one of the functions of the scene between Augusto Pérez and "Unamuno" in Chapter XXXI where the author assures for himself the durability of a literary character; the scene represents, as Blanco Aguinaga says, "one more effort to achieve some sort of immortality by making sure he appears in a realm where he will always be seen by mortals" (ibid., p. 204). He will make himself an object for his readers. Yet appearing in a novel means being fictitious; "Unamuno" becomes "something out of a book". In *Cómo se hace una novela*, Unamuno countered his fear of the insubstantiality of fiction by saying that everything is fiction and dream. That is also Víctor's advice and the novelist follows it.

Blanco Aguinaga maintains that Unamuno, "in spite of many statements to the contrary . . . was aware that Fiction is and always will be no more than an imitation of Reality". According to his interpretation, their confusion is only apparent; it is part of a complicated game through which the author hopes to "create free subjects in whom the reader can immerse himself while being aware that he – the reader – is giving them a life they do not have" so that he becomes aware of the creative act and therefore also of "the presence of an author who at no moment really vanishes from his work" (ibid., p. 204). I believe Unamuno's attempt is somewhat simpler and more quixotic, a serious effort to turn all reality into the author's fiction.

In shifting back and forth between objective reality and literary fabrication Unamuno works in the cervantine tradition, but with strategies more reminiscent of the character than of his author. Cervantes's vision is relativistic and illusionistic; Unamuno's is absolute and illusory. Cervantes, the humorist, plays upon man's varied interpretations of reality and his constant efforts at self-

[9] "My Eugenia, the one that I am forging on the fugitive vision of those eyes, of that pair of stars in my nebula."

deception. Unamuno moves from a mocking to a serious view of delusion and ends up affirming that reality is "really" illusion. He goes from comic exposure (*desengaño*) to philosophical entanglement (*engaño?*). Leo Spitzer wrote that Cervantes's perspectivism allowed him to stand above and sometimes aloof from the misconceptions of his characters. Unamuno enters *Niebla* to show his solidarity with Augusto Pérez. The real protagonist of the *Quixote*, Spitzer points out, is Cervantes, "the artist himself who combines a critical and illusionistic art according to his free will".[10] Unamuno certainly wanted to be the real hero of *Niebla*, but his intrusions aim at supplanting criticism with the affirmation of illusion.

For the Baroque artist, "disillusionment is allowed to color all things of the world, including books and their words which possess only the reality of a *sueño*. Words and books are 'sources of hesitation, error, deception – dreams' "[11]. Unamuno reverses the Baroque *desengaño*; as I said, he turns Calderón upside down, fusing novel, dream, and immortality into a single nebulous concept – "mist" –and then proclaiming this as the true "creative word".

In the prologue to the 1935 edition ("Historia de *Niebla*", II, 795-803) Unamuno examines the responsibility of the novelist in regard to the dreams of his readers. He says that although the reader does not like to have his "illusion of reality" taken away from him, it is the novelist's duty to do just that; only those who are conscious of dreaming are truly awake. He thereby implies that the oscillations and reversals of a work like *Niebla* make people aware of their tendency to replace the real with the imaginary. Fiction alerts one to the deceits of the mind, to the gap between words and things. Yet *Niebla* moves towards a conceptual mystification that seems to justify a dream-like vision of the world. The language of the prologue carries this mystification to an extreme. "Immortality, like the dream, is either communal or it is not . . . This is the mist, the nivola, the legend, this is eternal life – and this is the creative dreaming word." History, literature, and personal immortality combine in a single semantic cluster. Fiction becomes a refuge – a fantastic refuge.

*   *   *

San Manuel Bueno, mártir (*Saint Emmanuel the Good, Martyr*, 1931, XVI, 563-678) is another of Unamuno's most well-known works. For many readers it too is puzzling and somewhat anomalous in relation to the author's most frequently expressed views. An unbelieving priest in a remote provincial village devotes his life to preserving the simple faith of his parishioners; he manages to conceal his inner torment so successfully that everyone regards him as a true saint blessed with the grace of an unshakable faith. The story has been seen as a veiled confession of duplicity in which Unamuno gives aesthetic form to the revelation of his own disbelief. It has also been taken as evidence of a psychological transformation or of a deep spiritual crisis.[12] The man who con-

---

[10] "Linguistic Perspectivism in *Don Quijote*", in *Linguistics and Literary History* (New York: Russell & Russell, 1962), pp. 41-85.

[11] Spitzer, p. 185.

[12] See Sánchez Barbudo, "Los últimos años de Unamuno," in his *Estudios sobre Unamuno y Machado* and José Ferrater Mora, *Unamuno, Bosquejo de una filosofía* (Buenos Aires, 1957), p. 116.

stantly preached strife seems here to be proposing not just a truce but uncondi-tional surrender. The man who vehemently attacked "blind faith" ("la fe del carbonero") seems suddenly to be upholding the value of delusion. The Unamuno who took it as his personal mission to awaken the sleeping here creates a character who spends his life protecting the dreams of others. It looks as if the *agonista* has abandoned the battlefied to seek permanent solace in the countryside.

Other critics have pointed out that the reversal is more apparent than real. We should not let ourselves be misled by the conceit of an invented narrative into thinking that Don Manuel is his author's spokesman. His conflicts and doubts are the same as Unamuno's but they occur in the context of fiction. We are dealing with a novel and not with an essay that undisguisedly sets forth the writer's views.[13] In *San Manuel Bueno* the play between "fiction" and "reality" (between the story as told and its meaning) is at once elaborately complicated and naively obvious. That devious and artful play deserves our strictest attention.

The novella's opening sentence is one paragraph long; crowded with infor-mation, it presents the principal characters (priest, village, and narrator), fore-shadows the plot and its conclusion and gives the first taste of a confessional style that continually makes us aware of a writer who, already foreseeing the completion of her project, signs her first sentence with an author's pride.

> Now that the bishop of the diocese of Renada, to which this my beloved village of Valverde de Lucerna belongs, is seeking (so they say) to begin the process of beatification of our Don Manuel, of our Saint Emmanuel the Good, who was parish priest, I want to put down here, in the form of a confession (although to what end only God, and not I, can say), all that I know and remember of that matriarchal man who filled the most intimate life of my soul, who was my true spiritual father, the father of my spirit, of mine, of Angela Carballino.

The style, colloquial and laconic in Spanish, speaks the writer's absorption in her theme and recalls the unselfconscious fluency of St. Theresa (as Blanco Aguinaga says, "the classicism of the quotidian"). We also notice that, like St. Theresa, the writer explains her motivation in the most pious terms; it is the Lord who has, for some inscrutable reason, ordained this confession. She is truly inspired; her language comes to her from elsewhere and, like any good literary style, it implies more than it says. If Angela seems to take for granted that her reader knows as much about the protagonist as any inhabitant of the village ("our Don Manuel"), she nevertheless reveals, through the careful ingenuousness of her words, certain thematic connections which she (and Unamuno) would never make explicit but which determine the novel's whole design.

Unamuno, as we have seen, rarely used a first-person narrator; only, one might say, in moments of greatest stress – or of greatest command – did he resort to the story-teller's mask. In other novels he used it to describe the frenzied paroxysms of envy and self-hate. But here the tone is strikingly peaceful. The narrator appears at first to be one of Unamuno's gentle self-abnegating heroines.

---

[13] See Blanco Aguinaga, "Sobre la complejidad de *San Manuel Bueno, mártir*, novela", *Nueva Revista de Filología Hispánica*, 15 (1961) 572.

Since she is writing a memoir and not a drama, or even a novel, she favors her own reconstructions and nostalgic evocations over direct quotation and dialogue. Angela Carballino remembers what was said and she remembers what others told her was said. She strips those recollected speeches of dramatic actuality by certain repeated and timeless qualifying phrases – "he liked to say"; "he used to say"; "he often said". She does not give us an historical account but a reminiscence in which the past becomes part of a diffuse and indeterminate present. As Blanco Aguinaga has observed, the whole narrative is suspended in the imperfect tense; specific action blurs into the unvarying continuity of a monotonous and "eternal" daily life. The narrator's memory merges all past events in a single hovering and never-completed sequence. The preterite appears only in brief passages that tell the most extraordinary happenings, and even they quickly revert to the tense of the repeated and the customary. Renada (*re-nacida*: that which is forever reborn – or that which is doubly nothing) has an "intrahistory" but very little history.

The story is simple (as Unamuno says in the epilogue, "I know very well that in what is told in this tale nothing happens"); most of it recounts the life and works of Don Manuel. Woven into and around that account is the description of the natural setting, Valverde de Lucerna, a tiny village at the foot of a high mountain and at the edge of a bottomless lake. At the beginning Angela says the priest was "tall, thin, erect, and he held his head the way our Vulture's Rock holds its crest, and in his eyes you saw all the blue depths of our lake". The development of the plot is also the development of this central image that fuses priest, lake, mountain, and all the inhabitants of the village, living and dead, into a single entity whose different components mirror and reflect each other.[14]

Alongside the gradual unfolding of the metaphorical identification of priest and people and landscape is what we might call the individual or family drama of Angela Carballino and Don Manuel. That story starts with a barely insinuated rivalry and displacement as the girl's real parents give way before the dominating presence of the priest, the "matriarchal male". She refers to her actual father as "the other one, my carnal and temporal father" whom she hardly knew. "The other one", "el otro" is the tag for the rival in Unamuno's novels of envy and dissociation. Neither Angela nor her mother remembers much about that man ("Don Manuel, whom she, like everyone else in the village, adored, with whom she was in love – in a completely chaste way, of course – had erased the memory of the words and acts of her husband"). One figure appears on the scene as a potential intruder in the idyllic love-affair between villagers and priest (or between biographer and priest). "That was when my brother Lázaro, who was in America . . . made my mother send me to the con-

---

[14] When Don Manuel recites the Apostle's Creed, his voice merges with that of the whole congregation: "All those voices fused in a single one forming a mountain whose peak . . . was Don Manuel . . . and on reaching 'I believe in the resurrection of the body and in life everlasting!' his voice slid, as into a lake, into the whole people, and he was the one who was silent." At this moment Angela hears the church bells of the village said to be "submerged in the bed of the lake . . . submerged in the spiritual lake of our people; I heard the voice of our dead who were reborn in us in the communion of saints".

vent school so that I could complete my education outside of the village." But upon her return, the other world beyond Valverde de Lucerna quickly fades away into the same misty limbo as the memory of her father – "lost as in a dream at dawn and in the distance of remembrance". Don Manuel's presence blots out or absorbs any other reality, the village "was all Don Manuel; Don Manuel with the lake and the mountain".

The narrator draws a picture of total dedication. The priest's life was active, she says, not contemplative, given wholly to the care of his parishioners; he visited the sick, reconciled families, consoled the embittered, and helped the dying; he also worked with his hands, tilling the soil, splitting wood, making toys for children. Like Angela, he also wrote – letters as well as the memoirs of others; the active life includes "literary" acts, the preservation of lives in writing (this detail of plot thereby reproduces and alludes to the novel's own form). He even managed to teach the village idiot, Blasillo, who aped his every gesture and word. He is the priest's distorted double who wanders through the streets echoing his Good Friday prayer, "My God, my God, why hast thou forsaken me?"

Just as the lake reflects the village and, according to local legend, harbors in its depths a submerged village where the souls of the dead reside – three levels of reflection and duplication – so too Christ is mirrored in Don Manuel and the latter in Blasillo, in a figure that schematically represents Unamuno's theory of consciousness: the divine comprehension of Christ stands opposed to an "idiotic" (private and peculiar) unconsciousness, and in between the agonic consciousness of Don Manuel. Both three-leveled images suggest a self-contained, self-duplicating world, and both also point to separation from the outside world and from others. In the terrible privacy of Blasillo's idiocy we see the priest's own isolation magnified.

Yet that isolation conceals itself behind good deeds (as he says, he seeks to dull his pain with the opiate of ceaseless activity); desperation underlies altruistic dedication. He worked for the peace and happiness of the villagers because of his own fears. "Contentment with life comes before all else. No one should want to die before God wills." Suicide is a recurrent motif in his thoughts. So is solitude. The first is tied to the fear of the second. For solitude, as Unamuno so often said, breeds envy and self-hate; it can lead to both murder and suicide. "I should not live alone; I should not die alone. I must live for my people, die for my people. How can I save my soul if I do not save my people's?"

The possibility of communal salvation gradually emerges as the real, though not always acknowledged, goal of Don Manuel's efforts. Salvation in and through others reminds us of Unamuno's preoccupation with fame and the perpetuation of his image. Don Manuel, the priest who cannot believe in the resurrection of the flesh promised by the Church, attains, in the pages of Angela's memoir, the immortality of name and of fame. He lives on in the memory of his parishioners. "When I came to know the secret of our saint, I understood that it was as if a caravan crossing the desert with their exhausted leader, would take him on their shoulders as they approached the end of the journey, in order to carry his lifeless body into the promised land." Even the history of his inner strife, apparently lost in the idealized and distorting communal legend, endures in his biographer's literary creation. Don Manuel finds the ultimate validation that Augusto Pérez – and Unamuno – longed for.

"To be seen, to be admired, to leave a name", wrote Unamuno two years earlier in the prologue to *El hermano Juan,* where he described "true human history" as the history of warfare and strife that begins with fratricide. The "theater of history" opens when God "looks with favorable eyes on Abel's offerings". The desire to be seen and the humiliation of not being seen, lead invariably to spiteful seeing – envy, *invidere,* casting the evil eye. Envy and vanity, Unamuno explains there, are the motive forces of human history. They may also be the motive forces in the priest's life though they are so hidden that they barely break through to the surface of the narrative. The reader recognizes those themes through a chain of familiar associations. Thus Angela tells us that Don Manuel never preached against heretics, freemasons, liberals, or even atheists but against maliciousness and an "evil tongue". Envy, he used to say, is fostered by those who like to think themselves envied. And, at the very beginning of her narrative, she referred to the fact that though Don Manuel had distinguished himself in the seminary, he had turned down a brilliant career in the Church because he "wanted only to be a part of Valverde de Lucerna". We might guess that the priest, like the old poet and the school teacher of Carrasqueda, had a very personal knowledge of ambition and envy. But we must return to the story to see how this submerged motif is integrated in the novel's action.

The reciprocity and reversability of roles which for Don Manuel characterizes envier and envied can also be seen in the tie between Angela and the priest, between narrator and the person recreated in her memoir. Thus, although he is the matriarchal male, the mother-father, under whose "protection" she places herself, he is also her child. When she first confesses with him, she finds that her "doubts, sadness and anxiety" change to a pity that awakens her maternal instincts. "I was only a girl, a child almost; but I began to feel myself a woman, I felt in my entrails the juice of maternity, and finding myself in the confessional with that saintly man, I felt something like a silent confession of his own in the submissive whisper of his voice." She remembered his mother crying out to him in church one day "My son !", and henceforth she confesses to him in order to console him, usurping, in a sense, his mother's role – and also becoming his spiritual guide. One day it is Don Manuel who asks her to absolve him "in the name of the people". A shared submissiveness – and a shared dominion – makes each one alternately parent and child, priest and penitent. Angela never marries; the village is the convent in which she is both sister and abbess.

Since Angela is the one who writes the account, she describes the bond in terms of her own somnambulistic absorption. She lives in the magical aura of the priest ("those years passed as in a dream") and his image grows in her without her realizing it because he is so quotidian, "like the bread we pray for in the Our Father". She once had to cut short a trip to the city because "I was smothered in the city . . ., thirsty for the sight of the waters of the lake, hungry for the sight of the peaks of the mountain" – hungry above all for Don Manuel, whose absence seemed to call to her as if he needed her. In *Del sentimiento trágico* Unamuno described the mutual longing of God and man in similar language.

The balance of self-mirroring characters bound in mutual dependence is broken with the return of Lázaro from America. His entrance also signals a widening of the narrative focus; the changeless life of Valverde de Lucerna suddenly opens out to reveal the social situation of all Spain, its backwardness, poverty, and ignorance. And we almost catch a glimpse of the exploitative forces that foster that stagnation. But the Unamuno who rejected his early Marxism argues here, through the priest and through Angela, for the blessedness of holy poverty. Lázaro, who brings from the New World new ideas and a missionary zeal for reform, must be made to see the error of his ways; after all, he has returned from death. He who would lead the blind ("lazarillo" is a blind man's guide) must be made to see his own blindness. He appears as the spokesman of "civilization" who criticizes the brutalizing habits of country life. When he learns of the "total dominion" exercised by Don Manuel, the "saintly evangelical man", over his mother, his sister, and the entire village, he sees one more example of the mindless theocracy which rules Spain. Lázaro's historical consciousness stands opposed to the eternal unconsciousness of the village. He is an intruder, the "other one"; as the priest's rival for the devotion of Angela and of all the villagers, he makes the triangle. The ensuing struggle with Don Manuel and Lázaro's conversion represent both the reestablishment of a reversible duality and the reabsorption of history by "intrahistory".

As in Unamuno's other triangular situations the "other" covets not the possession but the possessor. He "burns" with desire to see and hear Don Manuel, to be close to him, to converse with him and come to know "the secret of that spiritual dominion over souls". Like Berta in *Dos madres,* he aims at the secret of mastery over others. Yet Don Manuel converts him with the revelation of another secret, the secret of his disbelief, and he enlists him as an ally in the continued deception of the people. The villagers, however, see only the "recovery" of a lost soul, the resurrection of Lazarus. They celebrate Lázaro's communion "before the entire village, with the entire village". The recovery also initiates a betrayal : "then, since it was dawn, a cock crowed."

Lázaro reveals to Angela the priest's secret; he repeats to her Don Manuel's own justifications. "It is not sham. 'Take holy water', as someone said, 'and you will end up believing' " (Unamuno thus ties together Blasillo's unthinking imitation of the priest and the recommendation of deliberate automatism of another "Blas", whom Unamuno often quoted, Blaise Pascal). Truth is so terrible that "simple people could not live with it". His mission is "to sustain the lives of his congregation, to make them happy, to make them dream themselves immortal." Lázaro fully subscribes to this program. "Let them live in the poverty of their feelings and not acquire expensive sufferings. Blessed are the poor in spirit !"

Intertwined with the story of desperation over loss of faith in God and immortality is, not surprisingly, another story about a hidden yearning for immortality's shadow and the passion to which it gives rise. We have seen the allusions to envy in Don Manuel's sermons and in his fear of solitude. In one of his conversations with Lázaro he speaks of how life is a continual suicide or a continual struggle against suicide. The peace and beguilements of nature offer the greatest temptation to self-destruction; the bottomless lake of the village lures him. Abruptly shifting to an apparently different theme, he talks about the dreadful secrets of the dying and how he has divined on countless death-beds the true cause of mortal illness, of the "tedium of life" – something "a thousand times worse than hunger". Don Manuel does not tell Lázaro what that dreadful secret is but the reader of *Del sentimiento trágico de la vida*, alerted by a single significant phrase, recalls that what was there described as "a thousand times worse than hunger" was "spiritual hunger" or Herostratism. Unamuno uses both terms as synonyms for envy.

Angela seems to know nothing about Don Manuel's struggle against pride and envy, just as the narrator-protagonist of "Don Sandalio" seemed to know nothing about the roots of his own tedium and misanthropy. The theme is so deeply buried that, as in "Don Sandalio", only its consequences can be perceived in the priest's manifest anguish over belief and deception. The need to be seen has turned into an all-pervading sense of abandonment because God does not see. God's absent gaze dissolves reality into illusoriness : contentment, says Don Manuel, is not for those who have seen God's face, not for those whose "dream of life God has looked upon with his eyes".

The priest's remedy for despair is, we have seen, the active life, even though he defines it in terms of death. " 'Let us continue, Lázaro, to commit suicide in our work and in our people, that they may dream their lives as the lake dreams the sky.' " Suicide is both death and life, alternately the gift of the self and the destruction of self. Or, as he had said to Angela, he must die for his people in order to save his soul. Don Manuel endures his martyrdom for the sake of salvation not just in the next world but in this one. Faced with the solipsist's terrible loneliness, which is both cause and result of a devastating envy (envy of others, envy of their faith, envy of God the Father, lust for glory – in this late novel, Unamuno's readers would know full well what sentiments must torment a man like Don Manuel), the priest preaches a creed of action and commitment. But commitment to deception. He will save his people by deceiving them. This man "without illusions" tries to maintain what he thinks are the necessary illusions of others. He wants to save himself in others and through others by spinning around them a web of pious deceit. And he would like to take refuge there from the outside world; he dreams of perpetual protection in the eternal unconsciousness of the villagers.

Unamuno's fusion of contraries operates on all levels in this work. Thus the priest's deception about his inner self guarantees the preservation of his legendary self. Lázaro's collusion is a betrayal both of his previous convictions and of the credulity of the people; he further betrays Don Manuel in revealing his secret to Angela, yet that revelation strengthens her belief.

The story of the priest's suffering contrasts with its descriptive and symbolic frame. His agonic struggle comes to us through the misleading calm of Angela's remembrance. Dramatically, the novel pivots at the very point of the priest's most suicidal despair, in the passage just discussed. No sooner does Lázaro tell his sister (and we must remember that hers is a second-hand account) about

Don Manuel's advice to "commit suicide in our work and in our people" than he moves to another very different memory. One day the two men saw a young shepherd girl standing on a rise of the mountain slope overlooking the lake, "singing in a voice fresher than its waters". The priest says "it is as if time had stopped, as if that shepherdess had been there always, just as she is, singing like that, as if she would be there forever, as she was when my consciousness began, and will be when it ends. That girl is a part of nature, not history – along with the rocks, the trees, the water." The passage makes an abrupt "contemplative" break to the sequential development of the "agonic" plot. Action gives way to quietude and, since the metaphorical fusion of village-lake-mountain-people-priest has by now become part of the very warp of the text, the scene marks the moment when Don Manuel's history begins to slip back again into a dream-like "intra-history".

The timeless world of "intra-history" is, we know, always tied to nature. Yet nature, for Unamuno, is alternately a refuge and a form of annihilation. Significantly, the motif of suicide here heralds the vision of the magical stasis of rocks, trees, water, song. The natural elements that first appear in the novel as the symbolic attributes of Don Manuel now suggest the dissolution of his consciousness. Landscape, largely absent from Unamuno's novels since *Paz en la guerra*, reappears here (and in "Don Sandalio") as the complement of the lonely subjectivity of the character; it plays a supporting role in his story, expressing both an identification with the natural world that preserves the priest's image and his disappearance in oblivion and unconsciousness. Nature, like a dream, serves alternately – and even simultaneously – as the realm of plenitude and of destruction – substance and absence. In any case it cannot be the setting of human action and achievement. Nature does not form a continuum with human history but stands as its antithesis.

The narrative marks the move from history to "eternity" as the priest becomes more and more submerged in the timeless reverie of Angela. "And time ran on and my brother and I noticed that Don Manuel's strength began to fail and he could no longer contain all the fathomless sadness that consumed him." It is in this context of resignation and dream that the "social question" makes its second and last appearance. Lázaro tells the priest about proposals for an agrarian syndicate : "A union, a syndicate? What is that? . . . Our kingdom, Lázaro, is not of this world." Religion, according to Don Manuel, should not try to right the economic and political injustices of this world : such practice would only cultivate the illusion that the whole ephemeral show has some finality. He counsels resignation and charity; even the rich, he claims, must resign themselves to their wealth. Why create a new society based on equality and the destruction of the class system if that will only heighten the tedium of life? "One of those leaders of what they call the social revolution has said religion is the opium of the people. Opium – opium – opium. Yes, let us give them opium so they can sleep and dream. I myself take opium through my mad activity. There is no other life but this one; may they dream it eternal, eternal for a few years."

Don Manuel preaches "the hypnotic sense of life" with such fervor that the individual drama is pushed into the background. Angela's own tormenting doubts (which reflect the priest's) give way to a trance-like absorption : "everyone around me seemed to be a dream." Even the concrete world can dissolve into solipsistic fantasy; when the priest tells her to pray for Christ, she asks if she must also pray for the lake and the mountain. "Could I be possessed?" And indeed she is – by the force that corrodes all sense of reality. Angela's story, Don Manuel's story, the story about priest and village, converge in the word-play of "life is a dream". "One is finally cured of dreams," says Don Manuel, "one is finally cured of life – and as Calderón says, good works and and good deceptions are never lost, even in dreams." The death of the priest (in "the bosom of the Holy Mother Church of Valverde de Lucerna") and later of Lázaro, who had carried on his work, reinforce the theme of communal salvation. Lázaro becomes one of "our saints", a link between the two Valverdes de Lucerna, the ancestral town at the bottom of the lake and the living one reflected in its surface. The lake, like nature in general, has two alternating and opposing meanings – the destruction of consciousness (suicide) and the preservation of a past that nourishes and sustains, a community of men living and dead.

Angela's memoir recoils now upon itself; she moves inward and meditates on the lesson she has learned. "He taught me to live, taught us to live, to feel the sense of life, to submerge ourselves in the soul of the mountain, in the soul of the lake, in the soul of the people of the village, to lose ourselves in them in order to remain in them." Hours, years pass unnoticed. "I lived not in myself but in my people and my people lived in me . . . I lived in them and forgot about myself." Yet the memoir tells us nothing about those acts devoted to others. It gives no picture of the daily life of the village; Angela's chronicle excludes everyone but the principal characters. She talks only about three people – Don Manuel, Lázaro, and herself, and the second two live only in relation to the first. Her mother, her father, Blasillo, the inhabitants of the village, appear only as the qualifying characteristics of Don Manuel; they are, like the lake and the mountain, aspects of his personality, metaphorical attributions. At the novel's end, as in the beginning, only two individuals fill the screen. The triangular motif that sometimes represents tension and sometimes complementarity (real father-Don Manuel-Angela; Don Manuel-mother-Angela; Don Manuel-Lázaro-Angela; Christ-Don Manuel-Blasillo; mountain-lake-village) resolves itself finally in the stable, indeed "eternal", trinity of Angela-Don Manuel-people (*pueblo*).

Throughout the novel narrator and protagonist (like the narrator and protagonist of "Don Sandalio") reflect and duplicate each other. They represent complementary parts of a single personality; internal conflict is expressed not through opposing doubles but in the anguish of each mirrored self. Unamuno's suggestion in the epilogue to "Don Sandalio" that the whole fiction could have been devised to present "a kind of clever autobiography", that Don Sandalio has set himself outside of himself in order to "better represent himself and at the same time disguise himself and hide his truth", might also be applied to Angela's memoir.[15] Though Angela is the "messenger" of another, of the

[15] This is, in a general way, the thesis of Sánchez Barbudo.

author, Miguel de Unamuno, who, in this novel's epilogue, takes care to remind his readers that his namesake is an "arch-messenger", Don Manuel (with his divine namesake and his idiotic double), Don Miguel, Angela – Lázaro too (the voice of "reason" and therefore of death) – all of them can be seen, to use the phrase from "Don Sandalio", as "figures in a hall of fogged mirrors". All parts of a single character.

The narrator closes her account with a description of the snow falling on the lake, the mountain, or the memories of her father ("the outsider"), of her mother, of Lázaro, of the village, of San Manuel, a snow that "blurs the outlines of things and erases shadows because even at night the snow illumines . . . I do not know what is true and what is false, nor what I saw and what I dreamed – or rather what I dreamed and what I merely saw – nor what I knew and what I believed". As so often happens in Unamuno's fictions, the wished-for end is a non-ending; everything returns to an original matrix that encloses all oppositions and obliterates all outlines – the snowy world where all colors fuse into white. Yet this last dazzling vision of nature suggests not so much a return home as a flight to an imaginary land purified of human concern.

The luminous dream also holds out the hope for the salvation of the writer's consciousness in the pages of a manuscript. "Nor do I know if I am transferring to this paper, white as snow, my consciousness which will remain in it, leaving me without it." Angela, the messenger, is not so self-abnegating after all; like her author, like the old poet, she ponders the chances of a literary perpetuation bought at the price of self-estrangement ("leaving me without it"). Yet the possibility of loss and salvation (death and resurrection) turns out to be – and we are not surprised by this last twist of plot and image – extremely precarious. Angela wonders if she might be merely "a dream within another dream".

The framing dream is, of course, Unamuno's own; in the epilogue he speaks in his own voice, extending his narrator's musings on wakefulness and dreams to the synonymous motif of reality and fiction. His novel, Angela's novel, is, he says, the most intimate and true story. "I know that nothing happens [nothing comes to pass] in this novelistic narrative – but I hope it is because everything remains in it, as the lakes and the mountains endure forever, and the blessed simple souls fixed firmly beyond faith and despair, sheltered in the lakes and mountains, beyond history, in the divine novel." Unamuno, who shows in the novel the self-delusions of the would-be deluder, now steps in to argue for the validity of the dream-like lyricism of his messenger. The narrative which had seemed to counter Angela's faith in salvation (whether through others, through works, or in the unconscious peace of nature) with the priest's anguished sense of forlornness and his pain at being forsaken by the Father, ends with the author's own expression of hope in an eternal illusion, a divine novel. What is one to make of this plea for the dream?

In a newspaper article published in 1933 and entitled, after the phrase in that concluding paragraph, "Simple Souls" ("Almas sencillas", X, 991-94), Unamuno wrote that the public's reaction to San Manuel Bueno made him realize once more the almost "insuperable difficulty" people have in separating artistic fiction from natural reality. But then he quickly grants that they are, strictly speaking, inseparable and goes on to talk about "the identity between reality and fiction, wakefulness and dreams". In spite of this reversal, which is clearly disconcerting, he carefully distinguishes in the essay between the author's voice and that of his characters ("The author does not speak through the mouth of his creatures – they speak through him"). Answering those who have criticized him for putting into his novels thoughts and feelings better kept secret from "simple souls" who cannot stand the burden of doubt, Unamuno energetically repeats the arguments of *Del sentimiento trágico* – one must awaken the sleeping who are dreaming the dream of life. "Metaphysical and religious anguish . . . is a terrible thing but it is preferable to limbo." And, he continues, the childish unconsciousness of the Spanish people is much more damaging than a tormenting inner anxiety. "Take away their religion, their limbo-dream . . . and they will give themselves over to another opium, the revolutionary opium of Lenin." The dream of an earthly paradise will replace that of a heavenly one. Desperation is far more valuable than infantile delusion because out of it come "the most heroic historical creations . . . the most un-believable beliefs". The article closes with " 'The truth shall make you free', says Holy Scripture".

The essay is almost as confounding as the novel's ending. I suggest the fol-lowing interpretation. Unamuno reminds us that *San Manuel Bueno* is a work of fiction. It is not Angela's fantasy, no matter how beguiled the reader may have been by that lyrical ending. If the truth is to set one free, we must know the boundaries between truth and lie and see the difference between dreaming and art, for although the second is made out of the first, the poet always re-mains, as Antonio Machado said, skeptical about the "reality" of his poems. In this essay, Miguel de Unamuno, in his own voice, seems to be indicating that his novel may describe not only "false" consolation but also the value of acts undertaken out of concern for others; Don Manuel's dedication to others justifies his deception. It may be that, beyond the multiple delusions of his characters, the author is pointing to the hopeful belief that what counts is action and not dubious and unknowable inner essence (the question of whether, as Angela suggests, Don Manuel is mistaken in thinking he is an unbeliever). Such a belief stands opposed, of course, to Unamuno's repeated affirmations that the real self is the one that is underneath the one that acts. It is a reasser-tion of his contrary faith that a person is the child of his deeds.

But then – once more we must return to the text – those deeds bear scrutiny. We should look at the priest's acts, at Angela's, and also at the author's, at his created work.

Don Manuel's personal creed is contradictory. He preaches the "joy of life" and a religion supposedly of this earth; he says that the real saint is the one who works for the happiness of others. When Angela is tormented by doubts about the existence of heaven and hell, he tells her to believe "in the heaven we see" (*cielo* is both heaven and sky). " 'Look at it' – and he showed it to me above the mountain and below, reflected in the lake." There is no other life, he tells Lázaro, but this one, "eternal for a few years". Such eternity would mean not delusion but liberation from the anguish of self and of time; it is not life-everlasting, but the abiding moment.

Yet at the same time that he preaches the joy of life, he separates himself, as does Angela, from certain worldly commitments. This novel was published together with two other works, "Don Sandalio" and "Un pobre hombre rico o el sentimiento cómico de la vida" ("A Poor Rich Man or the Comic Sense of Life") and in the prologue Unamuno compared Don Manuel and the protagonist of the last story, a bank clerk, Emeterio, who spends his life saving; he saves his money, his health, his feelings, himself. He evades the attractive young woman who pursues him and restricts himself to his job and a few "entertaining, inoffensive, honest and healthy games" (chess, cross-word puzzles, and word games). "Intimate and deep ties", says Unamuno, might be found between "the man who, renouncing reproduction, committed his whole life to the eternal health of his fellow men" and the man who did not want to commit himself to anyone or anything. There are indeed many parallels between the two; we might say that Emeterio is Don Manuel's comic double. He too likes the role of mediator; he would rather be a marriage broker than married; "it is more amusing to commit others." He likes to watch life, to look on. Looking, he says, is "more spiritual". He has even thought of becoming a priest so that he could hear confession and, as a friend says, "so that others would undress their souls" before him.

Don Manuel also wishes to save himself (in Spanish *ahorrar*, to conserve, and *salvar*, to save from danger or death, do not allow a pun Unamuno would have used). Since he would like to conserve and perpetuate his soul, his primary concern, in spite of all his practical works, is the spirit. And he sometimes talks as if he wants to save only the souls of others, not their bodies. In rejecting any socially effective means of improving man's lot in this world, he disdains the flesh, its pains and pleasures. Announcing that his kingdom is not of this world, he turns away from everyday work and happiness. This disdain is at odds with his dedication to the present life of the village. He sees heaven in the blue sky above the mountain, yet renounces the living bonds of ordinary, embodied existence.

' The contradiction consumes him (just as Emeterio "consumes himself"). Don Manuel's agony is caused not only by his lack of faith in the next life but also by the opposing pulls between faith in this life and its repudiation. Because he splits himself in two, the priest separates the spiritual from the social, the need for salvation from the need for bread. Though one could just as well say the reverse, that the alienation of our culture, the real divorce between all creeds and reality, splits him in two. His tragedy lies as much in this inner division as in his longing for personal immortality. Indeed, that ghostly longing is the other side of his renunciation of the earth; if we seek only the other world, we cannot live in this one. The "other life" is not daily life.

Yet Angela never describes the conflict in this way, and though we should not forget that her second-hand account of the priest's anguish is the only one presented, we know that certain omissions and silences point to sentiments she seems scarcely aware of. Angela tells us about Don Manuel's saintly self-abnegation but her narrative provides little anecdotal evidence of it; it is more a record than a recreation. The priest seems to slip away from us behind the idealized vision of his spiritual daughter. There is never any true exchange between the priest and his parishioners – he speaks, they worship, and an inviolable distance separates them, a distance duplicated in the relation between character and reader. He exists for us less as a literary personage who discloses himself through his actions and words, than as an exalted image in the mind of a narrator whose reliability we have every reason to question. Thus, although by Angela's account his conduct is almost tiresomely holy, the reader can perceive other shadings in his personality, modes of thought and behaviour that have their roots in envy and enormous ambition. The disparity between her ingenuous simplification (which sees only the conflict between charity and lack of faith) and the fuller human drama behind it, contributes to the novel's teasing ambiguity.

When Unamuno encloses Angela's narrative within his own, he shifts our attention from her idealized vision to his created work. Her fantasy becomes fiction. But not quite. Because her narrative is, after all, written by Unamuno and their voices are often indistinguishable. When he says that he put into this novel "all my tragic sense of daily life", we realize the anguish can never be resolved; Don Manuel's tragedy is also Don Miguel's. The author too is torn between illusion and life, between impossible belief and intolerable existence. And since he hates the middle ground, he can find no place to stand. Rejecting both the "opium" of religion and the "opium" of social change, he cannot see his way to either a faith or a society fit for this life. So, once more, he takes refuge in the dream. The fusion between characters and author completes itself in the epilogue when Unamuno repeats and affirms Angela's lyrical obfuscation – the hope for personal salvation through a novel meant to be "the divine novel". Insight tangles with illusion; the plea for a life turned towards the world gives way to the reflexive, self-protecting image of an eternal dream. Like Don Manuel, Unamuno would like to save himself, perpetuate himself, within the dream he offers to his readers.

*   *   *

"The most heroic historical creations have been achieved out of desperation; desperation has created the most incredible beliefs." Out of desperation come all of Unamuno's writings and that desperation sometimes breaks the bounds of art. Over and over he tries to contain his inner strife in the pages of a book, but since he lacked full confidence in the power of his art, he often violated the objectivity of his fictions to plead with the reader for his personal literary salvation. His unwillingness to trust the work and respect its autonomy explains the unevenness of his literary achievement. But he did commit himself to the writer's task. And when he succeeds – or partially succeeds – he does survive (as do his characters) embedded in the texture of a plot, in the language of description and the play of dialogue. Unamuno survives as a fabric of words, a cluster of symbols. His wish for personal immortality finds – in some, not all of his novels – a momentary fulfillment in fiction. Because we read it. In a way his dream comes true, not because fiction is a magical preserve where "nothing passes and all endures" but because it is language that moves and circulates between people; one man's imaginative creation awakens the imaginative response of others. Thus the solipsist's wildest dreams turn out to be shared in the literary act. He who would be all things and persons unto himself, makes out of that aspiration a dramatic model of human passion and thereby becomes, willy nilly, a person in the world. As a writer he becomes one man among others, neither God nor abandoned creature, neither master nor slave, but a partner to his reader.

Afterword

In its determined subversion of the concrete and objective in favor of an absolutism of the inner self, in its exaltation of spiritual suffering, in its justification of inconsistency and contradiction, Unamuno's work dramatizes the situation of those nineteenth and twentieth-century writers who, painfully aware of the widening split between the private world and the public one, ally themselves with the first. In their writings we find a defense of the "ideal" against the "real". The ideal, whether conceived in individual terms as pure subjectivity or in cultural terms as autonomous and immutable values, must be defended against historical reality. Although in *Del sentimiento trágico de la vida* Unamuno speaks of his terrible need to live and perpetuate himself in time, not in eternity, we have seen that over and over he seeks refuge in the idea of the eternal. Thus he presents the tasks and problems of human life as universal and timeless : we must always struggle against being smothered by the empirical self (the *costra* or shell); language, because it belongs to others, inevitably tends to congeal the living thought behind it; literature is alienation; since society and the individual are forever irreconcilable, we are forced into either isolation or hypocrisy. Because he sees it as "real" and eternal, Unamuno chooses the "self that is" over the "self that acts". Disdaining history as noise and fanfare, he postulates an eternal *intra-history*. But these choices mean the repudiation of action and of life with others. The "self that is" is a wishful dream and *intra-history* is a fantasy picture about community and continuity. We have seen how repeatedly the insufficiency of these private myths leads to desperate efforts to re-affirm the validity of action and of social relationships and how those efforts lead to other, equally untenable, conceptions – the world as theater, the individual as actor or hypocrite. Unamuno's alliance with the inner world sets off a perpetual oscillation that takes the place of any dialectical process.

We have considered the peculiarities of Unamuno's contradictory thinking but the dilemma that lies behind it is far from unique. His intellectual ties with Hegel, Kierkegaard, Carlyle, Nietzsche and the existentialists who came after him, as well as the thematic and technical parallels between his fictional works and those of writers like Pirandello, Gide, Huxley, Hesse, have been the subject of numerous essays. But those studies are rarely critical. Indeed, most of what has been written about Unamuno adds up to an enthusiastic chorus of praise. The Unamuno bibliography of the nineteen fifties and sixties shows the influence of existentialist fashion and jargon. Critics write about authenticity, about "passionate subjectivity" or the "heroic struggle" of "men condemned to live in agony", about the "will to be", the possibility of "self-creation" in the pages of a novel, and so on, as if these formulae in themselves constituted proof of Unamuno's value and of Spain's contribution to contemporary culture. It often seems as if the hispanists are telling us that Spain is not a backward country after all because Unamuno read Kierkegaard (in Danish) before other twentieth-century Europeans, because he anticipated Sartre and was a forerunner of existentialism. But we do not have to defend Unamuno's topicality or Spain's status as part of modern Europe. What we should consider is how his particular solutions to the problems of freedom, will, the self, estrangement, action vs. contemplation etc. show the hazards of those modes of thinking that exalt the private, the "passionate", the inner. If we relate him to existentialism, we should be able to point out the dangers of the idealistic tendencies of that movement which strike us so forcefully in Unamuno's version of it.

Unamuno's works show the intensity of the need for autonomy and freedom but not the actual and objective situations that constrain and deform that need. He displaces the conflicts of his time to a purely subjective plane where they are heightened and idealized. Thus instead of talking about the real limits to individual freedom and action, he speaks of how consciousness experiences its limitations by coming up against the existence of others and the fact of mortality. We have seen that for Unamuno consciousness is not a grasp of the world but the painful sense of not being everything and everyone, of not being God, eternal, ubiquitous, complete. The conflicts involved in relations with others are transformed into the clash of consciousness with an "otherness" that is an abstraction. Unamuno is not concerned with suffering on the material level. The man who says we should put salt and vinegar in the wounds of the soul and awaken our fellow men to spiritual suffering is concerned with issues far grander than those of ordinary, everyday historical reality. The actual structure of society is replaced by a simple division between those superior people who prove their human worth by intensifying the pain of consciousness and the others who, lacking that spiritual sense of touch, do not agonize over God and immortality. In Unamuno's view these "somnambulists" make the social world a falsification, a farce that poses a continual threat to personal integrity. Thus we see how a contradiction that has become acute at a given historical period, the split between the private and the social, is internalized and made abstract.

Unamuno goes further; identifying the psychological with the ontological, he elevates that internal dissension into the principle of all being. His interest shifts from the national and historical topics of *En torno el casticismo* to the subjective themes of the subsequent essays and the ontological concerns of *Del sentimiento trágico de la vida*. In this book he tells us that there is no other being but consciousness. Thus being itself is insubstantiality and radical insecurity. But a subjectivity that constitutes itself as absolute leads inevitably to mystification. We have seen that process in all of Unamuno's works. The writer who so constantly reiterates his need for substance and bulk, converts that need into an abstraction. The "man of flesh and blood" becomes a disembodied ideal. The "will to be" is inflated until it is a force that encompasses all life, the entire universe. Yet, as we have noted, it exists in a vacuum; it does not operate as will but remains a pure virtuality. In order to attain a god-like freedom, will is torn away from the concrete circumstances of action. The "self one wants to be" is idealized and set in opposition to the person who must live here and now and with others. Unamuno himself shows us how wrong he is in telling us that true freedom lies within. His exaltation of the will and of the inner self leads to a denial of the world and of any possibility of real freedom, that freedom which can exist only in community.

The writings of Unamuno also demonstrate how the denial of the world is closely tied to characteristic psychological events and their novelistic representation – fragmentation, doubling, the breakdown of the boundaries between self and others and between literature and life, dream and vigil. Sometimes he develops these themes as part of a novel or story but often enough he turns the novel or story into an argument about the relative values of the "real" and the "dreamed". On the level of fiction, obfuscation can easily appear as wilful playfulness or as a much-prized "esthetic ambiguity". Yet the inseparability of Unamuno's fictional and discursive prose compels us to take a more critical view of that ambiguity (and such a view might well be extended to those non-Spanish contemporaries with whom he is so often compared). We cannot, like Augusto Pérez or the Unamuno who defends him, accept the confusion of reality and fiction. "Los sueños, sueños son."

Bibliography

Unamuno, Miguel de, *Diario íntimo*, Madrid : Escelicer, 1970.
———, *Escritos socialistas: Artículos inéditos*, ed. Pedro Ribas, Madrid : Ayuso, 1976.
———, *Obras Completas*, 16 vols., Madrid : Afrodisio Aguado, 1958.
———, *Obras Completas*, Madrid : Escelicer, 1967.
———, *Recuerdos de niñez y mocedad*, Buenos Aires : Austral, 1952.

Abellán, José Luis, *Miguel de Unamuno a la luz de la psicología*, Madrid : Tecnos, 1964.
Alas, Adolfo, ed., *Epistolario a Clarín*, Madrid : Escorial, 1941.
Ayala, Francisco, "El arte de novelar en Unamuno", in his *Realidad y ensueño*, Madrid : Gredos, 1963.
Azar, Inés, "La estructura novelesca de *Cómo se hace una novela*." *MLN*, 85 (1970), 184-206.
Bécarud, Jean, *Miguel de Unamuno y la Segunda República*, Madrid : Taurus, 1965.
Benítez, Hernán, see Valenzuela Benítez, Hernán.
Blanco Aguinaga, Carlos, "Aspectos dialécticos de las *Tres novelas ejemplares*." *Revista de Occidente*, 19 (1964), 51-70.
———, " 'Authenticity' and the Image." In *Unamuno, Creator and Creation*, ed. José Rubia Barcia and M. A. Zeitlin, Berkeley and Los Angeles : University of California Press, 1967, pp. 48-71.
———, "De Nicodemo a Don Quijote." In *Spanish Thought and Letters in the Twentieth Century*, ed. Germán Bleiberg and E. Inman Fox, Nashville : Vanderbilt University Press, 1966, pp. 75-100.
———, "Interioridad y exterioridad en Unamuno." *Nueva Revista de Filología Hispánica*, 7 (1953), 686-701.
———, *Juventud del 98*, Madrid : Siglo Veintiuno, 1970.
———, "Sobre la complejidad de *San Manuel Bueno, mártir*, novela." *Nueva Revista de Filología Hispánica*, 15 (1961), 569-88.
———, *El Unamuno contemplativo*, México : Colegio de México, 1959.
———, "Unamuno's *Niebla*, Existence and the Game of Fiction." *MLN*, 79 (1964), 20-37.
Bleiberg, Germán, and Fox, E. Inman, eds. *Spanish Thought and Letters in the Twentieth Century*, Nashville : Vanderbilt U. Press, 1966.
Braun, Lucille V., " 'Ver que me ves', Eyes and Looks in Unamuno's Works." *MLN*, 90 (1975), 212-30.

Catalán, Diego, " 'Aldebarán' de Unamuno. De la noche serena a la noche oscura." *Cuadernos de la cátedra Miguel de Unamuno*, 4 (1953), 43-70.

———, "Tres Unamunos ante un capítulo del Quijote." *Cuadernos de la cátedra Miguel de Unamuno*, 16-17 (1966-7), 37-74.

Ciplijauskaite, Birute, *El poeta y la poesía*, Madrid : Insula, 1966.

Coromines, Pere, "La tràgica fi de Miguel de Unamuno." *Revista de Catalunya*, 18, 83 (1938), 155-70.

Crawley, A. E., "Doubles." *Encyclopedia of Religion and Ethics*, ed. James Hastings. Edinburgh : T. and T. Clark; New York : Scribner's, 1906-26.

Deutsch, Helene, *The Psychology of Women*. New York : Grune and Stratton, 1944-5.

Díaz, Elías, *El pensamiento político de Unamuno*, Madrid : Tecnos, 1965.

———, *Revisión de Unamuno*, Madrid : Tecnos, 1968.

Durán, Manuel, "La técnica de la novela y la generación del 98." *Revista Hispánica Moderna*, 23 (1957), 14-27.

Earle, Peter G., "Unamuno and the Theme of History." *Hispanic Review*, 32 (1964), 319-39.

———, "Unamuno : *Historia* and *Intra-historia*." *Spanish Thought and Letters in the Twentieth Century*, eds. Germán Bleiberg and E. Inman Fox, Nashville : Vanderbilt U. Press, 1966, pp. 179-86.

Eco, Umberto, *Opera aperta*, Milan : Bompiani, 1962.

Enjuto, Jorge, "Sobre la idea de la nada en Unamuno." *La Torre*, 9, 35-6 (1961).

Fernández y González, A. R., "Unamuno en su espejo." *Boletín de la Biblioteca Menéndez y Pelayo*, 17 (1966), 233-304.

Ferrater Mora, José, *Unamuno, bosquejo de una filosofía*. Buenos Aires, 1944. Translation cited, *Unamuno, A Philosophy of Tragedy*. Tr. Philip Silver. Berkeley : University of California, 1962.

Fletcher, Angus, *Allegory; The Theory of a Symbolic Mode*. Ithaca : Cornell University Press, 1964.

Freud, Sigmund, "Antithetical Meaning of Primal Words." *Standard Edition of the Complete Works*, XI, ed. James Strachey. London : Hogarth Press, 1955.

García Blanco, Manuel, "Don Miguel de Unamuno y sus poesías." *Acta Salmanticensia*. Filosofía y Letras, VIII. Salamanca : Universidad de Salamanca, 1954.

Girard, René, *Deceit, Desire, and the Novel*. Tr. Yvonne Freccero. Baltimore : The Johns Hopkins University Press, 1965.

Granjel, Luis, *Retrato de Unamuno*. Madrid : Guadarrama, 1957.

Guerard, Albert, ed. *Stories of the Double*. New York : Lippincott, 1967.

Gullón, Ricardo, "El Amigo Manso, entre Galdós y Unamuno." *Mundo Nuevo*, 4 (1966).

———, *Autobiografías de Unamuno*. Madrid : Gredos, 1964.

Hegel, G. W., *The Phenomenology of Spirit*. Tr. James Baillie. London : Allen and Unwin, 1931.

Ilie, Paul, *Unamuno, an Existential View of Self and Society*. Madison : University of Wisconsin Press, 1967.

———, "Unamuno, Gorky, and the Cain Myth : Toward a Theory of Personality." *Hispanic Review,* 39 (1961), 310-23.

Kermode, Frank, *The Sense of an Ending.* New York, London : Oxford University Press, 1966.

Kierkegaard, Soren, *Fear and Trembling and The Sickness unto Death.* New York : Doubleday, 1954.

Klein, Melanie, *Envy and Gratitude; A Study of Unconscious Sources.* London : Tavistock, 1957.

Kohlberg, Lawrence, "Psychological Analysis and Literary Form : A Study of of the Doubles in Dostoevsky." *Daedalus,* 92 (1963), 345-62.

Lacan, Jacques, *Ecrits.* Paris : Seuil, 1966.

Laín Entralgo, Pedro, *La generación de 1898.* Madrid : Austral, 1947.

———, *Teoría y realidad del otro.* I. Madrid : Revista de Occidente, 1961.

Laing, Ronald D., *The Divided Self.* London : Penguin, 1966.

———, *Self and Other.* London : Tavistock, 1961.

Livingstone, Leon, "The Novel as Self-Creation." In *Unamuno, Creator and Creation,* eds. José Rubia Barcia and M. A. Zeitlin. Berkeley and Los Angeles : University of California Press, 1967, pp. 92-115.

Machado, Antonio, *Juan de Mairena.* Buenos Aires : Losada, 1949.

———, *Poesías completas.* Madrid : Austral, 1940.

Marías, Julián, *Miguel de Unamuno.* Madrid : Espasa-Calpe, 1943.

Marichal, Juan, "La voluntad de estilo de Unamuno y su interpretación de España." In his *La voluntad de estilo.* Barcelona : Seix Barral, 1957.

Merleau-Ponty, Maurice, *Signs.* Tr. R. C. McCleary. Evanston : Northwestern University Press, 1964.

Meyer, François, *La ontología de Miguel de Unamuno.* Tr. C. Goicoechea. Madrid : Gredos, 1962.

Miyoshi, Masao, *The Divided Self; A Perspective on the Literature of the Victorians.* New York : New York University Press, 1969.

Moncy, Agnes, "La creación del personaje en las novelas de Unamuno." *La Torre,* 11 (1963), 145-88.

Morón-Arroyo, Ciríaco, "*Niebla* en la evolución temática de Unamuno." *MLN,* 81 (1966), 143-58.

Olson, Paul R., "The Novelistic Logos in Unamuno's *Amor y Pedagogía,*" *MLN,* 84 (1969), 248-68.

Ortega y Gasset, José, *Meditaciones del Quijote. Obras completas,* I. Madrid : Revista de Occidente, 1963.

París, Carlos, *Unamuno, estructura de su mundo intelectual.* Barcelona : Península, 1968.

Parker, Alexander A., "On the Intepretation of *Niebla.*" In *Unamuno, Creator and Creation,* pp. 116-38.

Pérez de la Dehesa, Rafael, *Política y sociedad en el primer Unamuno: 1894-1904.* Madrid : Ciencia Nueva, 1966.

Rank, Otto, "The Double as Immortal Self." In his *Beyond Psychology.* New York : Dover, 1958.

Reik, Theodor, *Masochism and Modern Man.* Tr. Margaret Boigel and Gertrud Kurth. New York : Farrar, Straus, 1949.

Ribbans, Geoffrey, "The Structure of Unamuno's Niebla." In *Spanish Thought and Letters in the Twentieth Century*, pp. 395-406.

———, *Niebla y soledad*. Madrid : Gredos, 1971.

Río, Angel del, Introduction to Unamuno, *Three Exemplary Novels*. Tr. Angel Flores. New York : Grove Press, 1956.

Rogers, Robert, *A Psychoanalytical Study of the Double in Literature*. Detroit : Wayne State University Press, 1970.

Rougemont, Denis de, *Love in the Western World*. Tr. Montgomery Belgion. New York : Doubleday Anchor, 1957.

Rubia Barcia, José, and Zeitlin, M. A., eds. *Unamuno, Creator and Creation*. Berkeley and Los Angeles : University of California Press, 1967.

Rudd, Margaret, *The Lone Heretic; A Biography of Miguel de Unamuno*. Austin : The University of Texas Press, 1963.

Salcedo, Emilio, *Vida de don Miguel*. Salamanca : Anaya, 1964.

Sánchez Barbudo, Antonio, *Estudios sobre Unamuno y Machado*. Madrid : Guadarrama, 1959.

Sartre, Jean-Paul, *Being and Nothingness*. Tr. Hazel Barnes. New York : Philosophical Library, 1956.

———, *Search for a Method*, Tr. Hazel Barnes. New York : Vintage, 1968.

———, *St. Genet*. Tr. B. Fretchman. New York : Mentor, 1964.

Serrano Poncela, Segundo, *El pensamiento de Miguel de Unamuno*. Mexico : Fondo de Cultura Económica, 1953.

Spitzer, Leo, "Linguistic Perspectivism in the *Don Quijote*." In his *Linguistics and Literary History*. New York : Russell and Russell, 1962, pp. 41-85.

Tuñón de Lara, Manuel, *Medio siglo de cultura española (1885-1936)*. Madrid : Tecnos, 1970.

Tymms, Ralph, *Doubles in Literary Psychology*. Cambridge, England : Bowes and Bowes, 1949.

Valenzuela Benítez, Hernán, "La crisis religiosa de Unamuno." *Revista de la Universidad de Buenos Aires*, 3, 9 (1949).

———, *El drama religioso de Unamuno*. Buenos Aires : Universidad de Buenos Aires, 1949.

Webber, Ruth House, "Kierkegaard and the Elaboration of Unamuno's *Niebla*." *Hispanic Review*, 32 (1964), 118-34.

Yglesias, Luis, "Alienation and the Poetic Word : A Study of the Poetics of Miguel de Unamuno and Antonio Machado." Unpublished dissertation. Harvard, 1968.

Zavala, Iris, *Unamuno y su teatro de conciencia*. Salamanca : *Acta Salmanticensia*. Filosofía y Letras, I. Universidad de Salamanca, 1963.

Zubizarreta, Armando, *Tras las huellas de Unamuno*. Madrid : Taurus, 1960.

———, *Unamuno en su nivola*. Madrid : Taurus, 1960.

Colección Támesis